THIRD EDITION

Career Success
The Attitude Advantage

Rosemary T. Fruehling, Ph.D.

Roberta Moore

Publisher
The Goodheart-Willcox Company, Inc.
Tinley Park, Illinois
www.g-w.com

To the Student

One of the most important factors in your success is your human relations skills, or your ability to get along with others. Human relations skills are a reflection of a person's attitude. If your attitude is positive and constructive, you will have a great advantage in work and in life.

Career Success: The Attitude Advantage is designed to introduce you to human relations skills and teach you the most important skills in a fun, easy-to-read format. Each chapter is organized into four easy-to-read and easy-to-understand sections: Case, Analyze, Apply, and Review.

"Case" is a realistic case study that opens each chapter. Case analysis questions follow, presenting you with an opportunity to give your opinion and record your reactions to the case.

"Analyze" examines the key concepts of the chapter and the relationship of those concepts to the case. Key terms in the Analyze section are highlighted in bold color and are defined in the glossary at the back of the book.

"Apply" is a new case to which you can apply concepts learned in the Analyze section. Discussion questions follow for another opportunity to record your impressions of the case.

"Review" provides an opportunity for you to review the concepts learned in the chapter.

This book was designed to help you learn how to interact effectively with others and to achieve success through a positive, constructive attitude.

About the Authors

Rosemary T. Fruehling received her B.S., M.A., and Ph.D. degrees from the University of Minnesota in Minneapolis. She taught office education at both the high school and postsecondary levels and conducted business education teacher-training. She was the manager of postsecondary vocational education for the Minnesota State Department of Education and director of software technology development for the State of Minnesota. Dr. Fruehling served as a consultant to many businesses and authored several business textbooks.

Roberta Moore received her B.A. degree from Wayne State University in Detroit, Michigan. She has comprehensive experience in trade, professional, and educational publishing. She was an editor and manager of vocational and business education publishing programs with McGraw-Hill and has worked as a consultant for other major publishers. Roberta has authored several business textbooks. She currently runs her own consulting business in publishing, marketing, and communications.

Contents

Part 1 Understanding Human Relations

MBI/Shutterstock.com

Part 2 Attitudes at Work

Branislav Nenin/
Shutterstock.com

Part 3   Succeeding on the Job

Flamingo Images/
Shutterstock.com

Part 4   Dealing with Problems on the Job

stokkete/Shutterstock.com

PART 1
Understanding Human Relations

MBI/Shutterstock.com

1 The Need for Human Relations Skills

Objectives

- Define human relations.
- Explain why you need human relations skills.
- Describe how human relations skills help you on the job.

Key Terms

interact
human relations
human relations skills
communication
verbal communication
nonverbal communication
body language
mixed message
self-awareness

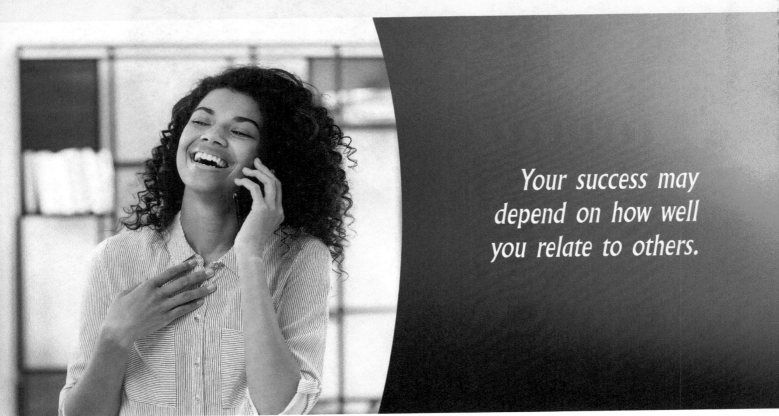

Your success may depend on how well you relate to others.

Vadym Pastukh/Shutterstock.com

Case

Does Anyone Really Work Alone?

"Hey, Wendy, you don't look happy," Len said as he sat down to join her in the cafeteria. "What's the matter?"

"Sometimes I have a habit of opening my mouth and putting my foot in it. I just made my friend Jessica upset by telling her she needs to stop tweeting and start studying," said Wendy.

"Well, doesn't she?" Len smiled. "You told me she said her grades are slipping."

"Yes, but she said journalism majors must keep up with what's happening at all times. I could tell she was angry. I wish I hadn't said anything. I need to brush up on my human relations skills—like knowing when to keep my advice to myself."

"Maybe so. But that's why I'm going into accounting," said Len. "I'll be all alone with my computer. No need to worry about getting along with people as long as my numbers are correct."

"Well, I'm going into computer technology, but no matter what you do, you still need to learn about human relations," said Wendy.

"What's to know?" Len asked. "You get along with people or you don't. People you don't like, you stay away from. The ones who don't like you leave you alone. It's that simple."

"I don't think so," Wendy said. "Maybe in your personal life, but at work you have to deal with people whether you like them or not."

"Not me," Len smiled. "I've got it figured out. I'm going into business for myself. I'm going to have a home office where I only interact with me, myself, and I."

Wendy looked surprised. "Are you kidding? How will you get business without interacting with your clients?"

"E-mail, texts, and social media. No need to talk."

"You'll see," said Wendy. "Even without face-to-face contact, you need to build positive relationships. You'll have to attract clients through networking and recommendations from satisfied customers. You can't do that by not caring about relationships. In fact, you'll have to care even more because you won't have a work group or supervisor or a company's reputation to support you."

"Hey, Wendy, you do give a lot of advice," Len said with a smile. "But I think it's good advice. I see your point, and I take it to heart. I'm going to have to rethink my ideas about studying human relations."

Case Analysis

After you have read the case *Does Anyone Really Work Alone?*, answer the following questions.

1. What is your reaction to this case?

_____

_____

_____

2. Which person's perspective on getting along with people best matches yours?

_____

_____

_____

3. Do you generally feel you need to like someone in order to get along with them? Why or why not?

_____

_____

_____

4. Do you want a career that involves face-to-face communication, or do you prefer to work alone most of the time? Why?

_____

_____

_____

5. What is your preferred way of communicating with people in your everyday life?

_____

_____

What advantages do you find with this method?

_____

_____

_____

What disadvantages do you find with this method?

_____

_____

_____

Analyze

You can have excellent job skills and still fail to achieve your career goals. You can also be honest and hardworking, but even that does not guarantee success. Why? The reason is that almost everything you do is affected by how well you interact with people. To interact means to engage with others through communication and behavior. The interaction of people with each other is called human relations. Human relations skills are the skills you use to make your interactions with people as positive as possible. These skills are a key factor in the success of most people in work and all aspects of life.

Why You Need Good Human Relations Skills

In a single day, you interact with many people—classmates, friends, instructors, family, and others. You may have casual interactions with salespeople, bus drivers, and others in your neighborhood. In many of these cases, you may not be aware of how others see you or how they feel about your behavior. At other times, you go out of your way to make a good impression. There are even times when you do not care what others think about you. No matter what you are thinking, how you relate to others affects everything that happens to you.

The study of human relations helps you understand why people behave the way they do. You will see why they think and feel the way they do. The study of human relations will also help you learn more about yourself. As you learn more about yourself, you will be able to adjust your behavior to improve your interaction with others.

Human Relations Is Communicating

Interaction between people involves communication, the process of sending messages from one person to another and receiving feedback. Communication involves talking, listening, writing, and reading. It also involves actions, such as rolling your eyes, winking, or waving. Communication is the essence of human relations.

Communication can be verbal or nonverbal. Verbal communication is communication using words. The impact and clarity of your communication depends on the words you choose. Whether others "get" your message depends on whether they understand your words and how they interpret your words.

Nonverbal communication is communication without words. Nonverbal communication includes gestures, facial expressions, and actions. Nonverbal communication is also called body language.

Sometimes nonverbal communication provides feedback more plainly than what is said. For example, if someone asks, "Do you understand?" and you say yes with a frown or confused expression, the person is more likely to "hear" the message sent by your facial expression. When your words and body language conflict, this is called a mixed message.

Even what you wear and how you walk communicate messages to others. Clothing and posture are part of nonverbal communication. For example, in some jobs casual attire is perfectly acceptable. On a job interview at a corporate office, the same clothes would communicate a different message. Regardless of what you have to say, in this setting the nonverbal message would be, "I do not fit in here."

Human Relations Is an Essential Job Skill

If you focus, as Len did, on work skills alone, you may find it much harder to succeed at work. On the other hand, you will probably have a hard time if you have no work skills, even if you are very charming. People who are all charm often manage to get others to do their work. In this way, the charmer may appear successful. Such a person is an example of the power of good human relations skills. Usually, the charmer's lack of skills is ultimately discovered.

For your best chance at success, develop your work skills and your human relations skills. Wendy had the work skills needed for the job. She also realized that an important part of her ability to succeed in her work is interacting with people. She understood that the two are closely related and cannot be separated.

Good Human Relations Requires Self-Awareness

At times, you are aware of what you are communicating to others. At other times, you are not. Being aware of how you communicate is an important step in developing good human relations skills. The next step is being aware of how people react to you. The combination of being aware of yourself and the reactions of others is called self-awareness. Being aware of yourself does not mean that you should constantly worry about what others think of you. It does mean that you need to think about how your actions are received by others.

Once you have self-awareness, you can develop skills to improve your communication. You can more consciously speak and act in ways that have a positive effect on people. The goal of good human relations skills is to have positive and constructive relationships. The cases in this book will help you achieve this goal.

Andrey_Popov/Shutterstock.com

Apply

Case: Human Relations at Work

bbernard/Shutterstock.com

Alexandra and Carlos have just been hired to work in a large office that has an open floor plan where workstations are arranged in cubicles along the walls on each side. Workers have little privacy in this setup, but, fortunately, the group gets along well with each other. They welcome both newcomers equally and offer to help them get adjusted. Alex is an outgoing person who enjoys talking and getting to know the new coworkers. Within a couple of weeks, she is joining members of the group for lunch, helping to organize the spring softball team, and sharing talk about what everyone did over the weekend.

Carlos, on the other hand, is somewhat shy and wary of getting too friendly with people at work. He also worries about what the boss might think of employees who spend time chatting instead of working. At lunchtime he prefers to take a walk to shop or do errands. He likes his coworkers but is just not that interested in their personal lives or forming friendships with them. The lack of private space and being expected to form new social relationships so quickly is causing him stress.

Case Analysis

1. What are the advantages of being like Alexandra?

_____
_____
_____

2. What are the advantages of being like Carlos?

_____
_____
_____

3. What are the drawbacks of being like Alexandra?

_____
_____
_____

4. What are the drawbacks of being like Carlos?

_____
_____
_____

5. At work, how much socializing is too much?

_____
_____
_____

Review

True or False

Indicate *T* if the statement is true or *F* if the statement is false.

1. _____ Almost everything people do in life is affected by how they relate to others.

2. _____ Human relations involves only the positive interactions with others.

3. _____ Communication is the essence of human relations.

4. _____ *Verbal communication* is another term for *body language*.

5. _____ Nonverbal communication includes the words a person says to others.

6. _____ Being aware of oneself as well as the reactions of others is called *self-awareness*.

7. _____ Self-awareness is a necessary part of good human relations.

8. _____ People with excellent work skills do not need good human relations skills.

9. _____ People can achieve success on the job without work skills if they have good human relations skills.

10. _____ The goal of human relations is to have positive and constructive relationships.

Check Your Understanding

1. Describe two different kinds of communication.

_____
_____
_____
_____
_____
_____
_____
_____

2. How can self-awareness help you improve your human relations skills?

_____
_____
_____
_____
_____
_____
_____
_____
_____

3. How do human relations skills help you on the job?

_____
_____
_____
_____
_____
_____
_____
_____

4. Why are human relations skills important for your future?

_____
_____
_____
_____
_____
_____
_____
_____

Journal Writing

1. Do you agree that it is important to get along with people in the workplace whether or not you like them? Why or why not?

_____

_____

_____

_____

_____

_____

_____

_____

_____

_____

_____

_____

_____

_____

_____

_____

2. Evaluate your own human relations skills. Are they good or poor? What do you think you need to improve?

_____

_____

_____

_____

_____

_____

_____

_____

_____

_____

_____

_____

_____

_____

_____

Name_____

With Whom Would You Interact?

The chart below lists a variety of careers. If the career you are interested in is not included, add it in the row at the end of the chart. If you had a job in each career, with whom would you interact? Place an X in the appropriate columns.

Career	Customers	Coworkers	Supervisor	People to Supervise	Upper Management	Others
Accountant for a Hotel Chain						
Administrative Assistant						
Airline Flight Attendant						
Auto Mechanic						
Computer Programmer						
Construction Worker						
Customer Service Representative						
Hotel Front Desk Manager						
Medical Lab Technician						
Photographer						
Receptionist						
Retail Salesperson						
Salesclerk						
Software Developer						
Stockbroker						
Telemarketer						
Other (please indicate): _____						

2   Your Attitude Counts

Objectives

- Understand how attitudes are formed.
- Explain the difference between a positive and negative attitude.
- Describe how attitudes affect behavior and how attitudes can change.
- Understand how attitudes affect the workplace environment.

Key Terms

attitude
positive attitude
optimistic
negative attitude
pessimistic
values
personality traits
group mentality

Your behavior is influenced by your attitude.

Jacob Lund/Shutterstock.com

Case

Does Being Nice Count?

"It's only 10 o'clock in the morning and I'm already having a bad day," Jonathan said to his cubicle mate, Samantha.

"Don't start, Jonathan, please. It's too early to have a list of complaints for the day." Samantha smiles and offers Jonathan a banana. "Here, have some calories. That always makes me feel better."

"Seriously, Samantha. Jen and I had a 9 o'clock meeting with the boss, and when I walked in at 8:55, there was Jen showing her the slides for the presentation that we had worked on together. I sat there feeling like I was late, which I wasn't, and feeling like an observer even though I had done half the work." Jonathan looked really defeated, and Samantha felt his pain.

"You just have to accept that Jennifer is extremely ambitious and smart. She knows how to get the attention that will get her ahead. Don't take it personally." Samantha advised.

"But I do because I believe in fairness and she doesn't care about anybody but herself. She takes all the credit and doesn't even thank me for sitting back and letting it happen. I'm trying to be nice about it, but she's not a nice person," Jonathan concluded.

"She may not be, but you need to learn to stop letting her get under your skin. Continue to do a good job and stop comparing yourself to Jen. Speak up for yourself. The boss is smart enough to recognize your worth, I'm sure. Everyone else does."

"You know, Samantha, you might have a point. I'm going to stop allowing myself to get riled up about Jen. Here I am wasting time talking to you about her instead of polishing that presentation so I can impress the boss. Thanks for listening, though," Jonathan said with a smile.

"No worries," said Samantha. "Talking things through helps. That's what friends are for."

Case Analysis

After you have read the case *Does Being Nice Count?*, answer the following questions.

1. What is your reaction to this case?

_____

_____

_____

2. Describe Jonathan's attitude about getting along with coworkers.

_____

_____

_____

3. Describe Jen's attitude about getting along with coworkers.

_____

_____

_____

4. Describe Samantha's human relations skills.

_____

_____

_____

5. What would you have done if you were faced with Jonathan's situation?

_____

_____

_____

6. What is a positive way for Jonathan to say something to Jen about her actions?

_____

_____

_____

7. What role could Jen and Jonathan's boss play in helping to encourage positive relationships?

_____

_____

_____

8. Some managers see competition among employees as a healthy way to get them to do good work. Do you agree or disagree? Explain your answer.

_____

_____

_____

Analyze

An **attitude** is a state of mind, belief, or feeling that causes you to act or react in a certain way. Attitudes reflect your feelings about things both large and small. We all know people we call "positive"—or maybe we describe ourselves that way. Across the spectrum is the person who is "negative"—always seeing the downside of things or taking things in a downward direction with their words or actions.

You may have a specific attitude about a person, situation, or idea. You may have a general attitude about life. Your attitudes often affect your behavior toward others. Some attitudes are flexible and easy to change. Others are strongly held and very hard to change.

Attitudes Are Learned

How are attitudes formed? Attitudes are usually developed over the years. You learn attitudes from family and friends; television, films, and other media; and through your life experiences and education. Your community and cultural background also have a strong influence on your attitudes. You can sum it up by saying attitudes are formed from all your experiences and are reflected in your personality and behavior. Whether your attitudes are positive or negative depends on what you experience and learn and how you react to that.

Attitudes Can Be Positive or Negative

Having a **positive attitude** means looking on the bright side of situations and interactions with people. Another word for it is **optimistic**, believing that, for the most part, life is good and expecting good things to happen. When problems occur, people with positive attitudes do not look to blame others. Instead, they try to take action to make things better. People with positive attitudes are usually upbeat and enjoy making others happy. They are the friends who make you laugh when you are feeling sad and the family members who help you find solutions to your problems.

Having a **negative attitude** means focusing on the bad aspects of interactions and situations. Those who are **pessimistic** believe that in most cases the worst is likely to happen. When problems occur, they look for excuses or blame others. They feel that they cannot do anything to make things better. People with negative attitudes may easily become angry or upset. They are the people who predict bad outcomes and leave you feeling gloomy when you tell them your problems. They have a hard time tuning in to the hopeful possibilities in life.

Attitudes are learned by imitation or reinforcement from family and social relationships. Like other things that we know and act on, they can be reinforced. The most powerful reinforcers of attitudes are social—your family, your friends, your coworkers, your community. Attitudes also change over time. Some of the most powerful agents of attitude change are learning new things and having new experiences. When you expand your knowledge and seek new experiences, attitudes that were reinforced by your family, close friends, and community will be influenced and may be changed entirely.

Having a positive attitude makes it easier to learn from both good and bad experiences. Optimism makes it easier to be open to making changes. Jonathan saw the negative side of Jen. He assumed he did not look good in front of his boss and focused on Jen's poor behavior. However, he was open-minded and willing to see things a different way after confiding in Samantha. He was willing to try to turn his attitude around.

On the other hand, Jen had a positive attitude. She assumed that her boss would think highly of her when she showed up early with a sneak peek at the presentation. Whether or not the strategy was working, Jen was being optimistic about her chances to get ahead. On the other hand, she also needed to think about having a positive relationship with her coworker.

Attitudes Reflect Values

Your attitudes reflect your values. Values are the standards you use for evaluating people and events and for making decisions about what is important to you. Experiences begin molding your values from the moment of your birth.

Here is an example: you go out to a restaurant with a group of friends or relatives and the service is terrible. The food is cold, they are out of the night's specials, and your table is located near the kitchen. Some of you will laugh it off and focus on enjoying each other's company. These are the people who value time spent with loved ones and see that as most important. Others will become angry and feel the evening has been spoiled. Their attitude reflects a focus on their expectations not being met. The tendency either to overlook adversity and see the bright side or to focus on the problem reflects a person's overall attitude. It is an indication of how they handle their feelings in general. In this sense, a positive or negative attitude is ingrained in their responses and can be seen as a personality trait. An individual's personality traits are the relatively stable, consistent, and enduring characteristics that form their patterns of behaviors, attitudes, and feelings.

Attitudes Can Change

Attitudes are formed over time, but they are not carved in stone. It is true that you cannot change your experiences, but you can change your attitudes about what you learn from them. You have the power to choose whether to see people and situations in a positive or negative light. You can change your attitudes to match the kind of person you want to be.

Make it a point to become more self-aware. Pay attention to how people respond to your words and actions and how it makes you feel. When you get a negative response, do you reflect on why you got that reaction? These observations can help you evaluate your choices and the attitudes behind them. Your evaluations can help you decide which attitudes are serving you well and which you want to change.

Education can lead to changes in attitude. Some negative attitudes are based on lack of information. Learning new information by reading novels, memoirs, biographies, and self-help books and articles shows you how other people think. As you learn more, you begin to understand different points of view. Your mind opens to new ideas, and your attitudes may change.

The natural progression of maturing and having new life experiences leads to changes in attitude. Teenagers value freedom and independence and may vow they will never give their child an early curfew or take the car keys away because of poor grades. When they have their own children, they realize the need to balance a child's independence with concerns about safety and well-being. The adult sees that their parents were not being too harsh. They were enforcing limits that were in the teen's best interests.

Attitudes Vary

Today's workforce consists of a diverse mix of people. You may find yourself working with people of different races, cultures, and religious backgrounds. You may work with people of all ages. Your coworkers may come from a variety of economic backgrounds or geographic regions. They might have widely different experiences, opinions, and attitudes. Human relations skills are essential in this type of workplace. To work together productively, people must cooperate despite their differences.

Adopt the attitude that differences present opportunities. People do not need to think or act alike to do a good job. Different opinions can lead to creativity and better problem solving.

Attitudes Show

Many supervisors are skilled in reading the attitudes of their employees. You show your attitude in many ways:
- in your approach to school or a job
- in your willingness to follow directions
- in the way you handle problems
- in your reaction to criticism
- in the way you relate to coworkers
- in the way you relate to people in authority

Attitudes Can Be Contagious

A positive attitude makes human relations much easier. It can be good for your career and your personal life. How? Positive attitudes can be contagious. People often respond to a positive attitude by becoming positive themselves.

Which classes do you most enjoy? Usually, they are the classes in which the instructor is enthusiastic about the subject and about teaching. When the instructor communicates a positive attitude about students' ability to succeed, students are likely to respond positively.

In your own life, which people are you most eager to see? Are you eager to see people with a positive attitude, full of fun and ideas? Do you want to spend time with people who have a negative attitude and are always complaining and discouraged? When you are negative, people tend to respond in the same way.

It is worthwhile to try to always have a positive attitude in your work environment. Even though a positive attitude may be hard to maintain, it will have an impact on your career. If you are energetic, motivated, productive, alert, and friendly, your coworkers and supervisors will respond positively to you. A positive attitude also will be transmitted to clients and customers.

The worker with a negative attitude may be unable to work well with others. Coworkers will tend to avoid interactions, and managers may see the negative person as a less valuable employee.

A negative attitude can spread through a group, causing workers to develop a negative **group mentality**. This is the tendency of the people in a group to think and behave in ways that conform. Members of the group reinforce each other's negative thinking rather than acting and thinking as individuals. An example is when workers fall into the habit of constantly complaining to each other about what they do not like on the job, rather than offering positive solutions. Productivity and the quality of work may suffer. Gossiping about coworkers and supervisors is another way that negative attitudes spread in the workplace.

On the other hand, a positive group mentality motivates the members and creates an atmosphere of support and enjoyment. Positive coworkers help each other and console each other when one of them feels down. They avoid gossip and treat colleagues and managers with respect.

michaeljung/Shutterstock.com

Apply

Case: A New Coworker

You have a part-time job in a large retail store. The job requires that you work closely with another coworker. The two of you have a lot in common—the same sense of humor, work ethic, and outside interests. You become good friends and look forward to going to work every day. You challenge each other and invent ways to increase sales in your department. Then your friend decides to leave for another job. You hope you will have an opportunity to build another good relationship.

fizkes/Shutterstock.com

Your new coworker is older than you and is used to doing things differently. The two of you do not share many sales strategies or interests outside of work. You miss your friend and are having a hard time working with this person. You begin to feel bored and cannot wait for the day to end. Your supervisor notices that you are not achieving the same level of sales as before and that you are losing interest. You are taken aside and told to "get back on the ball."

Case Analysis

1. List three options for dealing with your job situation.

_____

_____

_____

_____

_____

_____

2. List the option you would choose and explain why you would choose it.

_____

_____

_____

_____

_____

_____

_____

_____

_____

_____

_____

_____

Review

True or False

Indicate *T* if the statement is true or *F* if the statement is false.

1. _____ Attitudes are reflected in how a person interacts with others.
2. _____ Optimistic people have a positive attitude.
3. _____ Positive attitudes make it harder to learn new concepts.
4. _____ People can decide to change their attitudes.
5. _____ Attitudes are formed early in life and cannot be changed.
6. _____ Although education is important, it has little effect on attitude.
7. _____ Lack of information can cause a person to form a negative attitude.
8. _____ Diversity in the workforce makes human relations skills less important.
9. _____ Managers may see an employee with a negative attitude as less valuable to the organization.
10. _____ The attitude of a work group can lead to a negative or positive group mentality.

Check Your Understanding

1. Explain how attitudes develop.

_____

_____

_____

_____

_____

2. Describe a person with a positive attitude. Describe a person with a negative attitude.

_____

_____

_____

_____

_____

3. Give an example of how an attitude affects behavior.

_____

_____

_____

_____

_____

4. Give an example that shows how attitudes can change.

_____

_____

_____

_____

_____

Journal Writing

1. Describe a situation in which your attitude affected your human relations. Was the attitude positive or negative? What was the effect of this attitude? As you think about the situation now, what would you change?

_____

_____

_____

_____

_____

_____

_____

_____

_____

_____

_____

_____

2. What does it mean when someone says, "you have an attitude"? Describe a situation in which this was said to you or about someone else. What prompted the remark? Was any action taken to change the situation?

_____

_____

_____

_____

_____

_____

_____

_____

_____

_____

_____

_____

What Is Your Attitude?

Attitudes are formed over time, and they are complex. With new experiences and knowledge, attitudes can be changed. The following quiz will give you some insight into your attitude today. For each pair of statements, place an X by the one that more closely describes you. Respond honestly. This exercise is only for your own self-development.

A	Statement A	B	Statement B
	I listen to other people's ideas and weigh all sides in a discussion.		Other people's ideas are not as good as mine, so I do not usually give them much weight.
	I need to gather as many facts as possible before forming my opinions.		I know where I stand on most issues, so I have no need to explore the pros and cons.
	I feel comfortable speaking in front of a group to share my thoughts and opinions.		I am nervous speaking in front of a group. I feel that my opinion is not important to others.
	I enjoy meeting new people, both on the job and in social situations.		I avoid situations where I do not know most of the people.
	I try to understand the feelings of others and to respond to their needs.		It is impossible to understand every person, so I do not bother.
	I am patient with difficult people and try to work things out.		It is impossible to please difficult people, so I do not even try.
	I believe it is my responsibility as an employee to be loyal, even if I dislike my job or my boss.		A bad boss or a bad job deserves neither my respect nor my loyalty.
	I am comfortable working with people who do not share my background.		I am uncomfortable working with people who do not share my background.
	Having a good sense of humor is helpful when dealing with people on the job.		Work is serious business, and humor is out of place.
	Total As		**Total Bs**

Scoring

For each mark in the A column, give yourself one point. The B column marks get no points.
My total score is _____.

Interpretation

Score	Meaning
9 or 10	Congratulations! Your positive attitude will help you in any career you choose.
7 or 8	Your attitude is basically positive but could be better. You need to improve your attitude in one or two areas.
5 or 6	Your attitude is split between positive and negative and may be causing you problems. You need to improve your attitude in several areas.
4 or fewer	Your attitude is mostly negative and is probably causing you problems. Your attitude may also keep you from achieving success. You need to improve your attitude in many areas.

Action

It is always a good idea to work on improving your attitudes; but the lower your score, the more work you need to do. Below, list the problem areas you need to work on. For each problem area, describe one way to improve. Focus on one area for at least a week. When you have improved in that area, work on another. Continue until you think you have improved in all your problem areas. If your score is 6 or below, you might want to meet with an instructor or counselor to discuss ways to improve your attitude.

Ways to Improve My Attitude

_____
_____
_____
_____
_____
_____
_____
_____
_____
_____
_____
_____
_____
_____
_____
_____
_____
_____
_____
_____
_____

3 Teamwork

Objectives

- Understand the value of teamwork in the workplace.
- Explain the meaning of being a team player.
- Describe what individuals contribute to a team.

Key Terms

team
teamwork
productivity
team player
cooperation
talent
skill

When people work well together, everyone profits.

Gorodenkoff/Shutterstock.com

Case

Can Teamwork Save the Day?

Will is head of Communications at a large hospital. He is happy with the teamwork of his staff members Tanisha, Kevin, and Jackie. Tanisha is the senior member of the department. She develops community outreach and educational programs. Kevin handles social media and staff communications. Jackie is the newest member of the team, hired to assist where needed.

A few months after her arrival, Will saw that Jackie is a stronger writer than Kevin. Kevin's writing had been worrying Will. Now he has found a solution. At his weekly staff meeting, Will presented an idea.

"All of you have been doing excellent work. We're getting positive feedback all around. Jackie, your e-mails to the staff are striking just the right tone in clearly explaining the new procedures the hospital put in place."

"Thank you, Will," said Jackie. "I love writing and would like to do more."

"Well, that's just what I was thinking," said Will. Then he turned to Kevin. "Kevin, I would like you to work with Jackie on the newsletter with the idea that she will take it off your hands in a couple of weeks. I want you to focus more on public health programs and media coverage. These are your strengths."

Kevin was surprised. "Well, okay, if that's what you want. Sure, I'll work with Jackie and help her take it over."

"That's great, Kevin," said Will. "That's the kind of teamwork I expect in this department."

"That sounds great," Tanisha said. "In fact, would Jackie have time to do more postings about my programs on Twitter and Facebook?"

"Maybe I should do that while Jackie writes the newsletter," Kevin suggested. "After all, the interviews with staff and features take a lot of time."

"Oh, I don't think so, Kevin. We want the tone to be the same for all our communications, and that is Jackie's strength," Will replied with emphasis.

After the meeting, Kevin pulled Tanisha aside. "I'm very upset! Will should have talked to me first instead of announcing this in front of everyone. I felt I had to agree."

"Well, he's the boss and he's usually fair," Tanisha pointed out. "He probably assumed you'd be in agreement."

"Really? When he practically said outright that he likes her writing better than mine?"

"Kevin, you're great at speaking and working with the media and Will recognizes that. Jackie is more talented with written communications. I'm sure Will didn't mean this as a criticism of you."

"If you say so," Kevin said, but afterward he begins to avoid Jackie. She is aware that Kevin is unhappy, but it annoys her that he is taking it out on her. She needs information from Kevin to do her work. Jackie asks Tanisha to get the information for her. Tanisha understands how both Jackie and Kevin feel. She is caught in the middle.

Now everyone is unhappy. Tanisha does all she can to avoid taking sides and encourages the two of them to iron out their differences.

Jackie makes the first move. She invites Kevin to meet and starts by telling him how she feels. "I didn't make the decision to change your job," she says, "so I don't think it's fair that you're taking it out on me." Kevin is surprised and also relieved to have the chance to clear the air. He apologizes and decides that maybe it's time to have an honest discussion with Will as well. He knows Will is aware that the team has fallen apart.

Case Analysis

After you have read the case *Can Teamwork Save the Day?*, answer the
following questions.

1. What is your reaction to this case?

_____

_____

_____

_____

_____

2. Would Kevin have felt better about Will's decision if it had been
discussed privately first? Why or why not?

_____

_____

_____

_____

_____

3. What would you have done in Jackie's situation?

_____

_____

_____

_____

_____

4. Is it wise for Kevin to have a follow-up discussion with Will or
should he just let it go? Explain your answer.

_____

_____

_____

_____

5. What should Will do to get his team working together again?

_____

_____

_____

_____

_____

Analyze

Organizations have goals they need to achieve. That is the way they stay in business. A hospital needs to provide quality care to its patients. A police department must make the community safe for its citizens. A retail store must have products that appeal to its customers.

Employers want workers who work together to achieve these goals. Working together can be difficult when the interests of individual workers clash. When people get along and help each other get the work done, everyone profits.

Teamwork Increases Productivity

A successful organization is like a well-oiled machine. When all its parts work together smoothly, it runs at maximum capacity. In work organizations, individuals must work together in similar fashion. In today's organizations, this process is not just expected, it is formalized in a concept called teams. A team is a group of people who work together for a common goal. Teamwork is the activity of people working together to produce results that achieve the organization's goals. Many companies are now using Microsoft Teams and other similar platforms to support this way of working.

The goal of most organizations is to efficiently produce and deliver their products or services. Efficiency is usually measured by the amount of work done within a given period of time. Productivity is a measure of efficiency as defined by the organization's expectations of its workforce.

Employees who get their own work done efficiently are valued. Those who are willing to help others are even more valuable. Working together increases the productivity of everyone. High productivity is the goal of most work groups.

Team Players Help the Team

Jackie is a team player—a worker who acts to help the team succeed as a whole. Every team member is responsible for the success of the team. Teams are successful when each individual works to full capacity. To be most successful, the members of the team must be able to trust and depend on each other.

Jackie is practicing an important human relations skill: cooperation. Cooperation means working together for the common good. It is the key to good teamwork. Cooperation among group members increases productivity in many ways. Group members
- share information
- help each other solve problems
- work together to improve quality and reduce errors
- motivate each other to work smarter
- inspire each other to come up with better ideas

Jackie could have adopted the attitude that she was better than the other workers. Instead of talking with Kevin, she could have gone to Will to complain about Kevin's behavior. She could have pointed out that Kevin seemed to care more about his ego than about the work. Jackie's personal productivity would have been high. With Tanisha's help, she would have been able to get the work done in spite of Kevin, but the productivity of the group would not have improved. Tanisha might have been disappointed that Jackie complained to Will instead of trying to work things out with Kevin as she had advised. Tanisha and Kevin would probably have started to resent Jackie and worry that Will was favoring her. Their attitude toward their work might have become negative. As a result, their productivity would have decreased. The hospital Communications department would have needed a teamwork transfusion!

Individual Talents Create Strong Teams

What is talent? This term is not easily defined so experts constantly redefine it. However, a good working definition of talent is a unique pattern and combination of abilities. Talent is often thought of as the kind of ability that one is born with, although study and practice enhance talents and make them stronger. Talent is often contrasted with skill, which is an ability that requires development through study and practice.

As a member of a work team, you will find that your fellow workers have different talents and skills. Some workers have great writing ability.

Bitchayaarch Photography/Shutterstock.com

Others are good with facts and figures. Some people see the big picture. Others focus more on details. Some are very quick, while others need more time. When individuals contribute their unique talents and skills, the team is stronger and more capable of producing the desired outcome within the time allotted.

Even if you work mostly by yourself, as part of an organization, you are still a member of the overall team. Your job may be different from your coworkers who do team projects, but you may need to be a team player when it comes to other situations. Examples of this include coordinating lunchtime schedules or vacation leave, offering to pick up lunch for someone who has a deadline, or volunteering for a special project or event.

Apply

Case: How to Get Ahead

NDAB Creativity/
Shutterstock.com

You are the newest person to join the sales and customer service team at a retail clothing store. Your three coworkers have been working there for several years. You want to learn the job as quickly as possible and hope your supervisor will notice your skills and potential. By the second week on the job, you realize that your teammates' productivity is low. Often, while you're helping a customer, you see other customers looking around for help. Your coworkers are nowhere to be found. Customers often leave without buying or come to you when you are helping someone else. You see that you can easily outperform your coworkers, but the business is suffering.

Case Analysis

1. List two options for dealing with your job situation.

_____
_____
_____
_____
_____
_____
_____
_____
_____
_____
_____
_____

2. List the option you would choose and explain why you would choose it.

_____
_____
_____
_____
_____
_____
_____
_____
_____
_____

Review

True or False

Indicate *T* if the statement is true or *F* if the statement is false.

1. _____ When people get along and help each other get the work done, everyone profits.
2. _____ When working as part of a team, a person helps other team members only when that person's own work is done.
3. _____ High productivity is the goal of most work groups.
4. _____ Teams are more productive when each individual works to full capacity and helps other team members.
5. _____ Highly productive employees are not expected to help their coworkers.
6. _____ A good team player solves problems with coworkers.
7. _____ Interactions among workers affect group productivity.
8. _____ Cooperation among workers is necessary for high group productivity.
9. _____ Sharing information is not a good way to get ahead at work.
10. _____ Even those who work alone need to be team players to achieve work success.

Check Your Understanding

1. Why is cooperation an important human relations skill?

_____

_____

_____

_____

_____

_____

_____

_____

2. Describe a team that you have worked on or observed; for example, school council or a sports team. Give an example of cooperation on this team.

_____

_____

_____

_____

_____

_____

_____

_____

3. How does teamwork help increase productivity?

_____

_____

_____

_____

_____

_____

_____

4. Describe a team player.

_____

_____

_____

_____

_____

_____

_____

_____

Journal Writing

1. Name a team or a group to which you belong. Describe your contribution to the team and how it affects the team's productivity.

_____

_____

_____

_____

_____

_____

_____

_____

_____

_____

_____

_____

_____

_____

_____

_____

2. What talents and skills do you bring to a team?

_____

_____

_____

_____

_____

_____

_____

_____

_____

_____

_____

_____

_____

_____

_____

Communicating with Teams

How well do you communicate with others? The following quiz will give you insight into the communication skills that team members need. For each pair of statements, place an X by the one that more closely describes you. Respond honestly. This exercise is only for your own self-development.

A	Statement A	B	Statement B
	I feel comfortable asking a coworker or fellow student for help with a work problem or school assignment.		I have a hard time asking others for help.
	I feel confident speaking in front of a group.		Speaking to people in groups is hard for me.
	I explain things well. People understand what I am saying.		People often misunderstand me when I am trying to make a point.
	I engage with others in a group and do my share of the talking.		When in a group, I tend to keep quiet and take notes or just listen.
	In a group or at a meeting, I feel comfortable expressing my opinions and sharing ideas.		I often feel uncomfortable sharing my opinions and ideas in front of a group.
	People feel comfortable talking to me.		People rarely start conversations with me.
	I listen carefully when someone is asking me a question.		I often find myself thinking about how I will answer a question, rather than listening carefully.
	I think about how I am coming across when I disagree with someone.		I am usually pretty forceful in letting someone know when I disagree.
	I feel comfortable expressing myself face-to-face with others.		I would prefer to send a text message or e-mail.
	I am open to accepting other people's ideas or ways of doing things.		I tend to follow my own path because I'm usually right.
	Total As		**Total Bs**

For each mark in the B column, consider how the behavior might negatively impact your teamwork. You might want to consult a friend or family member to test your opinion of how you come across and get suggestions for ways to improve. You can also look at role models, such as people in your personal life—in school, work, or social situations—whom you admire, and work on emulating their communication style.

4 Relationships with Coworkers

Objectives

- Explain how relationships at work affect your happiness and success.
- Describe a good coworker relationship.
- Explain how relationships affect others in the workplace.

Key Terms

coworkers
peers
subordinates
hierarchy
impartial
oversensitive

Good communication is the key to positive coworker relationships.

Case

The Resentful Coworker

Roberto, the assistant business manager of a housing construction company, breathes a sigh of relief as he finishes an important proposal.

Roberto's supervisor, Harold, who usually writes the proposals, is out of the office on a work site. Sharon, the owner of the company, asked Roberto to fill in. He sees her coming and calls out, "Hey, Sharon! It's done! I can't wait to have your feedback. With fewer new houses being built, I know the company really needs to win this contract."

"It had better be good," Sharon says, smiling. "If we don't get this contract, there will have to be some layoffs. I'll look at it right away and send it this afternoon."

Roberto feels a little nervous. "Don't you think Harold should look at it first?" he asks.

"Harold is tied up with problems at the Main Street site," says Sharon. "I have confidence in you—and me. Let's go for it." She looks directly at Roberto and gives him a nod to show her sincerity.

Roberto feels proud. This is a stepping stone for him, and he is happy to see that Sharon has confidence in his work.

The next day, Sharon calls a staff meeting and announces that she hand-delivered the proposal to the head of the city housing authority and she is optimistic about their chances "thanks to Roberto's great work on the proposal."

Later, Roberto heads outside for lunch. It looks like everyone is picnicking outdoors on this beautiful, sunny day. He joins his coworkers, and they all congratulate him on Sharon's comments—all except Harold. Harold does not return his greeting or even look at Roberto. This worries Roberto, and as the group returns to work, he calls out, "Hey, Harold, hold on." Harold turns and waits for Roberto to catch up.

"Are you mad at me?" Roberto asks. "I felt like you were ignoring me at lunch. Did I do something wrong?"

"Do not act all innocent with me!" Harold replies angrily. "I came in today to work on the city proposal and discovered you'd already finished it. What's the big idea? Are you trying to steal my job?"

"Hey, slow down!" Roberto is surprised by Harold's anger. "I was not trying to do anything to you. Sharon said you were tied up and she asked me to pick up the slack. That proposal was a top priority and you know it."

"Well, you certainly didn't waste any time taking over," Harold countered. "And what? Are you calling me a slacker now?"

"Certainly not! Poor choice of words. I've been helping you prepare proposals for months now. You've been a great teacher. Don't you think it's time for me to have a chance to show what I know?" Roberto asks.

"I'm not sure you're ready for such a big responsibility," Harold says.

"Believe me, Harold, I'm not trying to steal your job. Sharon relies on you and we all know it."

"Maybe you're right. I guess my issue is really with Sharon. Why didn't she let me know she had given you the assignment?"

"I don't know, Harold. I think she was just focused on the need to meet the deadline and thought you were tied up. Maybe you should talk to her."

"No, I think I should just drop it. I should not have blamed you, though. It wasn't your fault."

Roberto feels a little puzzled. It was not exactly an apology, but he offers his hand in truce. The two men shake hands and walk inside with Roberto wondering if Harold no longer trusts him.

Case Analysis

After you have read the case *The Resentful Coworker,* answer the following questions.

1. What is your reaction to this case?

_____
_____
_____

2. What is the root cause of the problem between Harold and Roberto?

_____
_____
_____
_____

3. How did Harold communicate his feelings to Roberto?

_____
_____
_____
_____

4. What would you have done in Harold's situation?

_____
_____
_____
_____

5. Would you describe Roberto's response to Harold as constructive? Why or why not?

_____
_____
_____
_____

6. What do you think Sharon could have done to prevent the conflict between Harold and Roberto?

_____
_____
_____
_____

7. Do you think Roberto and Harold will be able to repair their relationship? Why or why not?

_____
_____
_____
_____

8. What can Roberto and Harold do to get their relationship back on good terms?

_____
_____
_____
_____

Analyze

Coworkers are people who work together within a department or work group and others with whom they interact in the workplace. When relationships at work are good, you are likely to be happy and more productive. When you are productive and happy, your chance for career success increases. When relationships at work are bad, you are likely to be unhappy and less productive. When you are less productive and unhappy, your chance for career success decreases.

In your social life, you choose your relationships. In your working life, however, you have no choice. You must work with the people on your team. You must learn how to develop good coworker relationships.

What Is a Good Coworker Relationship?

You do not have to be best friends with your coworkers. It is not even necessary to like your coworkers. However, you do need to work positively with everyone at work. You need to get along with your coworkers so that company goals are reached. You need to interact with your coworkers in ways that do not cause tension, anger, or conflict. A good coworker relationship has these characteristics:

- positive
- pleasant
- productive
- cooperative

People who work well together accomplish company goals. They also accomplish their own goals to be successful at work. They are able to talk openly about work and work-related issues with their coworkers. They can give and accept constructive criticism and resolve conflicts without anger and resentment.

Types of Relationships at Work

People who work at the same job level are called peers. In many companies, especially large ones, most interactions are with peers. Workers also interact with people in the job levels above them, such as supervisors, managers, and executives. These relationships are likely to be more formal. The staff members who work under the authority of the managers and supervisors are their subordinates, sometimes also called direct reports.

The ranking of workers based on the level of their jobs is called a hierarchy. No matter where a person is in relation to you in the hierarchy, you must treat everyone with respect.

Good and Bad Relationships Can Create Problems

How you feel about each of your coworkers is influenced by your personal likes and dislikes. Your personality and your attitudes will fit better with some people than with others. How others feel about you is affected in the same way. However, keep in mind that the reason for good relationships at work is to achieve company goals. Your success depends on the ability to interact with everyone in a positive way.

If you dislike someone, you are likely to create tension with that person. You may not even be aware of the tension you are causing. You may avoid each other, which may keep both of you from achieving work goals.

Sometimes, friendships at work can also be a problem. If you spend a lot of time talking about matters not related to work, you are not accomplishing work. You are wasting company time and risk being judged critically by managers or coworkers. Friendships can also cause jealousy and feelings of resentment if workers feel left out of a close-knit group. Friendships between managers and their subordinates are particularly tricky, as this can give the appearance of unfairness, whether or not it exists.

Relationships Can Affect Others

Coworker relationships do not exist in a vacuum. If two people become close friends, a third may feel excluded. If two people are angry with each other, the third may feel forced to take sides. Such situations distract all three people from getting work done.

Sharon's decision created tension between Roberto and Harold. Their lack of communication threatened to interfere with the department's work. Sharon was caught in the middle. She has a good relationship with each of them. Her behavior was **impartial**, meaning she was not showing favoritism toward or taking sides with either of her subordinates. She was feeling pressured to get the work done and did not expect her decision to cause problems. If Harold had continued to react angrily, such behavior could lead Sharon to question his ability to work well with his peers.

Harold's decision to "drop it" and not continue to blame Roberto for what happened is an example of good human relations. When peers talk to each other and resolve problems without complaining to their manager, they are showing their ability to work well together.

Take Responsibility

You are responsible for the quality of your relationships. When you see a way to improve them, take action. Do not wait for the other person to make a move. Quite often, the other person is unable or unaware of what must be done.

When Roberto saw that Harold was acting negatively toward him, he took the first step to improve the situation. Harold was angry, but once Roberto reassured him, he saw the situation in a different light. When they are both feeling more comfortable with each other, they will be able to reestablish the trust that Harold might have questioned. They should discuss their relationship and the need to work together to make the company stronger. In doing so, they will also make themselves more valuable employees.

Communication Is the Key to Good Relationships

Communication is the key to good relationships, at work and in your personal life. When relationship problems occur, communication often clears the air. However, you should avoid discussing issues in person or sending written messages when you or the other person is angry.

It is a good idea to let some time pass before sending a message or talking with someone when you or the other person needs time to calm down. Taking time to figure out what the real problem is, what is causing the behavior, and what the best solution is will usually bring about a better outcome for both of you.

At times, it is better to let things slide and not take any action. Avoiding action is most appropriate when you are being oversensitive, which means you are too easily upset, angered, or offended. In other words, no one has done anything wrong, but you react as though they have. Taking someone's actions or words personally when they were not intended that way is showing oversensitivity. It is sometimes hard to determine when you are overreacting. To help see the situation more clearly, it is helpful to talk with someone outside the situation, such as a trusted friend or coworker.

Generally, it is a good idea to think things through and make sure you are calm before you discuss work-related problems with your supervisor.

fizkes/Shutterstock.com

Natalya Stepowaya/
Shutterstock.com

Apply

Case: Working with Slackers

You are the most productive worker in your department. You enjoy your job and have good relationships with your coworkers. You sometimes find that you need to help them with their assignments. Lately, they need your help more and more. You wouldn't mind this so much if they were working hard. However, you are beginning to realize that they are slacking off because you have been bailing them out. You want to stop doing so much extra work.

Case Analysis

1. List three options for dealing with your job situation.

_____
_____
_____
_____
_____
_____
_____
_____
_____
_____
_____
_____
_____

2. List the option you would choose, and explain why you would choose it.

_____
_____
_____
_____
_____
_____
_____
_____
_____
_____
_____
_____
_____

Review

True or False

Indicate *T* if the statement is true or *F* if the statement is false.

1. _____Relationships with coworkers can influence your productivity.
2. _____A person must like everyone at work.
3. _____The result of good working relationships is achieving personal and company goals.
4. _____It is okay if people do not like all their coworkers, as long as they have positive relationships.
5. _____Coworkers whose jobs are at the same level are called peers.
6. _____Friendships at work never cause problems.
7. _____Relationships at work have no effect on career success.
8. _____Talking directly to coworkers about problems is a constructive way to solve conflicts.
9. _____Communication is the most important element in developing good relationships.
10. _____When someone is being oversensitive and has not been wronged, it is better if they do not take action.

Check Your Understanding

1. Describe a good workplace relationship.

_____

_____

_____

_____

2. Describe how relationships with peers can affect your happiness and success at work.

_____

_____

_____

_____

3. What does it mean to be oversensitive when you have a workplace relationship problem?

_____

_____

_____

_____

Journal Writing

Think of a relationship you have with a coworker, classmate, or teammate. Is the relationship good or bad? Give your evidence. How does this relationship affect your effectiveness at work, in school, or on the team? If the relationship is causing problems, what can you do to improve it?

_____

_____

_____

_____

_____

_____

_____

_____

_____

_____

_____

_____

_____

_____

How Do You Relate to Coworkers?

Choose two people with whom you have worked on a job, at school, through volunteer work, or on some other project. They should be your peers (at the same level as you). Coworker A should be a person with whom you have a good relationship. Coworker B should be a person with whom you have a poor relationship. Read each of the statements below. For each coworker, answer *yes* or *no* in the appropriate column.

Statement	Coworker A (good relationship)	Coworker B (poor relationship)
A good relationship with this person is important to me.		
My productivity depends on my relationship with this person.		
I lose my patience with this person.		
I think it is this person's responsibility to make the first move.		
Other supervisors favor me over this person.		
Other supervisors favor this person over me.		
This person often complains.		
This person has a positive attitude.		
This person does a good job.		
This person shares my sense of humor.		
We are about the same age.		
We can discuss problems honestly.		
We have similar backgrounds.		
We have similar beliefs and values.		
We have the same interests and lifestyle.		

Analysis

1. Compare your answers for Coworker A with your answers for Coworker B. Indicate the statements for which you answered differently for each coworker.

2. From these differences, why do you think you have more trouble relating to Coworker B?

_____

_____

Action

What can you do to improve your relationship with Coworker B?

Ways to Improve My Coworker Relationship

_____

_____

_____

5 Relationships with Supervisors

Objectives

- Explain the nature of supervisor–employee relationships.
- Describe how good coworker and supervisor relationships work.
- Understand the impact of supervisor–subordinate relationships on worker attitudes and productivity.

Key Terms

supervisor
manager
job performance
job satisfaction
subordinate

performance goals
jealousy
favoritism
mentor
merit

Relationships with supervisors affect your career success and coworker relationships.

Stock Rocket/Shutterstock.com

Case

The Problem with Favoritism

Jay recently joined the graphics department of a large advertising firm. The manager, Enrique, called his team together in his office on Jay's first day and introduced him.

"I want you all to welcome Jay to the group and make sure he succeeds," Enrique said. "Tamara will be his mentor to make sure he receives the coaching he needs to get up to speed."

Jay said, "Thanks, everyone, I'll appreciate your help. I've known Ricky for years, but the rest of this is all new to me." The meeting ended, and Jay stayed behind for a few more words with Enrique.

Some eyebrows were raised as the team walked back to their workstations. "Ricky?" Tamara asked. "That's cute. Should we all start calling him that?"

James pulled Tamara aside and whispered, "Just between you and me, I heard that Enrique and Jay's dad went to college together and that's why Jay got the job. They're buddies."

"Oh, great," Tamara expressed surprise. "And here I was thinking Enrique was fair and honest. Now he's hired some kid who's known him for years. Let's see how that works out."

Up to now, the workers in the graphics department have seen Enrique as a fair and honest boss. They appreciate that he does not play favorites. They all know they can go to him with a problem, and he will do his best to solve it. They have good coworker relationships and are happy in their jobs.

Jay makes a good impression. He is quick to ask questions and thankful for advice from his more experienced coworkers. They can see he will be an asset to the department, but they feel they are now at a disadvantage.

Jay sometimes mentions that he and Enrique get together to play basketball or attend sports events with Jay's dad. After a few months, when a new account is acquired, Enrique asks Jay to head the project. He has valid reasons for doing so. Jay recently worked at a firm that handled this same type of product advertising. However, Jay's coworkers see it differently. They are sure that Enrique has assigned the job to Jay because of their friendship.

"I trained him, and now he's getting the next new project," Tamara complains to Janine, another coworker.

"Yeah," says Janine. "Next thing you know, he'll be promoted over you."

"What's that supposed mean? Enrique has never been like that," Tamara insists. "I think he's a fair boss."

"He was up until now, before his 'favorite' got here. Now these guys are going to stick it to us. That's how the game is played."

The employees' jealousy begins to affect their relationships with Jay. They begin to see him as a threat to their careers. They are short with him when he comes to them for advice. They stop asking him to lunch with them. Jay feels excluded and cannot figure out why. He has no idea what he has done to upset his coworkers.

Their anger interferes with their previously excellent relationship with Enrique. They no longer see him as fair and impartial. Enrique hears the grumblings. He observes that the others are avoiding Jay. He is displeased with the decline in teamwork. He had thought everything was going along so well. What is wrong?

Case Analysis

After you have read the case *The Problem with Favoritism,* answer the
following questions.

1. What do you think is wrong?

_____

_____

_____

2. How would you describe the relationship between Enrique and the
staff before Jay was hired?

_____

_____

_____

3. How would you describe the relationship between Enrique and the
staff after Enrique and Jay started socializing outside of work?

_____

_____

_____

4. What is your opinion of the reaction of Jay's coworkers after Jay was
assigned the new project?

_____

_____

_____

5. How did the change in attitude of the staff affect the department's work?

_____

_____

_____

6. Do you think Enrique made any mistakes in his relationship with
Jay? Explain.

_____

_____

_____

7. What can Enrique do to improve his relationship with the staff?

_____

_____

_____

8. What can Jay do to improve his relationships with his coworkers?

_____

_____

_____

Analyze

Your relationship with your boss can have a big impact on your success and happiness at work. In the workplace, the terms **supervisor** or **manager** are the more formal terms used. These titles describe the same function, which is to manage the work of one or more employees. Supervisors and managers assign and evaluate employees' work and manage the day-to-day operations of work groups. They also make hiring decisions and set goals for their work groups. They are responsible for monitoring **job performance**, the assessment of how well employees perform their job duties and what areas need improvement or development.

Supervisors make many decisions that affect **job satisfaction**, the degree to which employees enjoy their work and feel a sense of achievement. Supervisors may influence opportunities to advance; for example, making decisions about whether you get training opportunities and are given the type of work assignments that will advance your growth. Relationships with supervisors and with coworkers have much in common. Both depend on effective communication between two people. However, there are some important differences.

Supervisors Set the Tone

Supervisors are responsible for setting the tone of the relationship with their subordinates. **Subordinates** are the workers who are under their authority. Some supervisors behave almost like coworkers. They socialize with their employees and treat them almost as peers. Others are all business.

Some supervisors are very good managers. Others are promoted to management jobs with little talent for the role. Some organizations provide training for new managers. However, many managers have no training in working with employees.

No matter what your supervisor is like, you must do your share to have a good relationship. Like all relationships between two people, it is a two-way street.

One critical role of supervisors is to make sure employees understand what is expected. Expectations encompass day-to-day work tasks as well as broader goals that daily work achieves. Many organizations require supervisors to set specific performance goals for each employee. **Performance goals** are work-related objectives that an employee is expected to achieve within a set period of time. They let employees know what is expected and how their work will be evaluated. Usually, performance goals are set annually and may be related to salary increases and promotional opportunities. Large organizations tend to have this type of structured program for setting expectations, while smaller ones may be more casual. In either case, as an employee, you have the responsibility to make sure you know what is expected of you. If you are ever in doubt, take the initiative to discuss expectations with your supervisor.

Environments Vary

Some organizations are informal. At those organizations, managers are flexible about time, dress, and behavior. There may be few rules, as long as everyone gets their work done. Other organizations are more formal. They may have a dress code and strict rules about behavior. The workplace environment typically depends on the type of business or service conducted. For example, a bank usually has a formal atmosphere. A software development business might be more casual.

The personality of the department manager will also be a factor. You need to recognize what type of supervisor you have. Are they someone who is lenient with employee behavior as long as the work gets done or someone who sets strict rules for behavior? Observing the way other employees interact when you start a new job is one important clue. Being alert to nonverbal communication will also give you clues.

The status of employees is another environmental factor to consider. In some organizations, high-level staff members are friendly with each other but more formal with subordinates. When you enter a new workplace, noticing these things will help you adjust your behavior. Being able to adjust to fit in is a good human relations skill to have.

Supervisors Should Be Fair

In the case, you saw how a relationship with a supervisor could be almost too friendly. Jay's friendship with Enrique ruined his good relationship with his coworkers. It is natural for employees to have different relationships with the boss. Supervisors like some people more than they like others. However, a supervisor–subordinate friendship that creates jealousy is a problem.

Supervisors and employees need to be aware of how workplace friendships can affect others. An overly strong friendship with a boss can weaken coworker relationships when it causes jealousy among coworkers. Jealousy is the feeling of hostility toward someone believed to be a rival or toward someone perceived to be getting special treatment or advantages. While jealousy is a fairly common emotion in everyday life, in the workplace it can breed the kind of negative group mentality you learned about in Chapter 2.

A manager must also avoid favoritism—showing special attention to someone in a group of people who are all supposed to be treated equally. Enrique's staff saw him giving extra attention to Jay. The staff saw them socializing outside of work. Jay then got the plum project. Enrique's behavior looked like favoritism. To some extent, it does not matter whether it really was or not. The appearance of favoritism is almost as bad as actual favoritism.

Enrique needs to work on his relationships with the other workers. He needs to act in a way that does not favor Jay or appear to favor Jay. He should help all staff members understand their jobs and do them well. He should be a mentor to each subordinate. A mentor is a person with experience who supports and advises someone with less experience to help them develop.

Jay needs to spend time with his coworkers and let them know that he is a hard-working member of the team. He will have to prove that he is getting ahead on merit—the actual quality of his work—and not because of his friendship with Enrique. Jay is finding out the potential problems with a social relationship with a supervisor.

As you work on having good supervisor–employee relationships, do not neglect your coworker relationships. Your success in your career and the productivity of your department depend on both relationships being good.

fizkes/Shutterstock.com

CREATISTA/Shutterstock.com

Apply

Case: Under New Management

On your previous job, everyone was friendly and at ease. Your supervisor was a fair boss and also a coworker and friend. When problems arose, the team solved them together. You felt free to walk in anytime and talk to your supervisor about work issues and always got a helpful response. Your job satisfaction was very high.

When a promotion opened up in another department, your supervisor acted as your mentor and encouraged you to apply. You got the job, but now you are having trouble adjusting. The work is satisfying, and your coworkers are pleasant. The supervisor, however, is very formal. You have to make an appointment to talk about work. There is never any social chat or interest shown in you as a person. Problems or questions are handled at a weekly staff meeting. At these meetings, the supervisor does most of the talking. You feel as if your ideas are not considered. You are wondering if you can ever make progress or be happy working for a supervisor who sets this type of tone.

Case Analysis

1. List three options for dealing with your job situation.

_____
_____
_____
_____
_____
_____
_____
_____

2. List the option you would choose, and explain why you would choose it.

_____
_____
_____
_____
_____
_____
_____
_____
_____

Review

True or False

Indicate *T* if the statement is true or *F* if the statement is false.

1. _____ Good relationships with supervisors are essential to progress on the job.

2. _____ All organizations give managers formal training.

3. _____ Organizations have different standards for dress and behavior.

4. _____ The supervisor sets the tone for the relationship with subordinates.

5. _____ Effective communication is less important in relationships with supervisors than with coworkers.

6. _____ Nonverbal communication provides clues about the tone of the work environment.

7. _____ An overly friendly relationship with a boss can create problems with coworkers.

8. _____ A mentor helps workers make progress on the job.

9. _____ Judging an employee "on merit" means judging on quality of work.

10. _____ How workers relate to supervisors is much more important than how they relate to their coworkers.

Check Your Understanding

1. Describe a good supervisor–worker relationship from a coworker's viewpoint.

_____

_____

_____

_____

_____

_____

2. How is a supervisor–worker relationship different from a coworker–coworker relationship?

_____

_____

_____

_____

_____

_____

3. Imagine you have a supervisor who is unclear about what is expected of you. Your work assignments are not explained, and your questions get vague answers. What would you do?

_____

_____

_____

_____

_____

_____

4. How does favoritism by a supervisor create problems in a work group?

_____

_____

_____

_____

_____

_____

5. How can a good relationship with your supervisor help you at work and in your career?

_____

_____

_____

_____

_____

_____

Journal Writing

1. Think of a personal experience with a supervisor or person in authority, such as a teacher, instructor, team captain, parent, or head of a group to which you belong. Describe the tone set by this person. Do you think it was/is positive and helpful to you? If not, what would you change?

_____

_____

_____

_____

_____

_____

_____

_____

_____

_____

_____

_____

2. What is your opinion of favoritism on the job or in school? Is it ever beneficial? If you have ever shown favoritism to someone, explain why. Describe a situation in which you have experienced favoritism or been affected by favoritism shown to someone else. What is the best way to handle favoritism?

_____

_____

_____

_____

_____

_____

_____

_____

_____

_____

_____

_____

_____

How Do You Communicate with Supervisors?

How well do you communicate with your instructors, supervisors, or others in authority? The following quiz can give you some insight. Think of a situation in which you are the subordinate. Read each statement below. Place an X in the "Agree" column if you agree. Place an X in the "Disagree" column if you disagree.

Agree	Disagree	Statements
		1. If I don't understand what is expected of me, I ask for more information.
		2. I feel comfortable asking for help when I need it.
		3. I expect to earn the rewards of working by doing a good job.
		4. I welcome having others criticize my work and point out how to improve it.
		5. I am willing to ask how I can improve my performance.
		6. I make it clear that I have personal goals and ambitions.
		7. I know how to tactfully say I disagree during a discussion with someone in authority.
		8. When my supervisor asks for my opinions, I am able to give them.
		9. If I am having a problem that affects my work, I can discuss it with my supervisor.
		10. I understand the difference between a good working relationship and a friendship.

Scoring

Count the number of statements for which you marked in the "Agree" column. This number is your score.

My score is _____.

Interpretation

Score	Meaning
10	Congratulations! You have almost perfect communication with your supervisor.
8 or 9	Your communication is good.
6 or 7	Your communication is average, but could be improved.
5 or lower	You need to work on ways to improve your communication.

Action

It is always a good idea to work on improving your communication; but the lower your score, the more work you need to do. Below, list the problem areas you need to work on. For each problem area, describe one way to improve. Focus on one area for at least a week. When you have improved in that area, work on another. Continue until you think you have improved in all your problem areas. If your score is 5 or lower, you might want to meet with an instructor or counselor to discuss ways to improve your communication.

Ways to Improve My Communication with Supervisors

PART 2
Attitudes at Work

Branislav Nenin/Shutterstock.com

6 Destructive Attitudes

Objectives

- Understand the nature of destructive attitudes.
- Describe the negative effect of destructive attitudes on the job.
- Define types of destructive attitudes.
- Develop awareness of your own destructive attitudes.

Key Terms

service industry
bigot
prejudice
racism
ageism

sexism
discrimination
oversensitivity
selfishness
dissatisfaction

No matter how negatively you feel about others, do not let it show in the workplace.

mavo/Shutterstock.com

Case

The Too-Efficient Server

As she is clearing away the dishes, Shirley collects her tip. "I knew they were going to leave a small tip," she says to herself. "I cannot stand these people with nothing better to do than shop and eat lunch. They should try working for a living, standing on their feet all day, and waiting on people who look down on them."

Shirley walks into the kitchen muttering to herself. José, the chef, asks her what the problem is, but she gives him a look that clearly says, "Don't bother me."

José shakes his head. Shirley has not forgiven him for the mistake he made last week. He mixed up her order with Felicia's. He overheard her telling Felicia, "That José doesn't even try to improve his English. I can't stand these people who come here and think they don't have to learn our language." It still upsets him to think about it. He was glad Felicia defended him by telling Shirley that it was an easy mistake to make.

The lunchtime crowd is slow today. Lately, business has been dropping off because regular customers are going to other restaurants in the neighborhood. As Shirley waits on her tables, she can hear Felicia laughing with a group at a table across the room. "Honestly," Shirley grumbles, "you would think she's here to have fun instead of work."

Shirley just wants to get people in and out as quickly as possible. She believes this is the sign of an efficient server. Most of the time, she does not worry about whether the customers like her. "Oh, sure," she thinks, "it's worth giving a little extra personal service to the businessmen. They have the money to tip well."

"Why does Felicia waste her time talking with those bums?" Shirley wonders. "They're not going to leave a big tip. And those senior citizens! If they're too broke to tip, they should just stay home. Most of them can't read the menu, so you have to keep repeating it to them. Good thing they don't sit in my station anymore," Shirley decides.

At the end of the shift, Dimitra, the restaurant manager, calls Shirley into her office. As soon as the door closes, Shirley begins complaining. "When Felicia lets customers linger over their coffee, I end up with more people at my station. It's not fair, and…"

"That's enough, Shirley." Dimitra stops her in mid-sentence. "As you know, our business is off. I have to let one server go. I'm afraid it's you."

"What are you talking about?" Shirley is stunned. "I'm the fastest server you have! I never make mistakes. I get people in and out quickly. Felicia is not as good as I am."

Dimitra nods. "You are efficient, but your attitude upsets the customers and staff. Felicia knows how to treat people so they want to come back. You, on the other hand, let your negative attitude affect your service. You almost chase people away. That's why I'm letting you go."

Name_____

Case Analysis

After you have read the case *The Too-Efficient Server*, answer the following questions.

1. What is your reaction to this case?

_____

_____

2. How would you describe Shirley's attitude toward her job and her customers?

_____

_____

3. How did Shirley's attitude affect her job performance?

_____

_____

4. Do you agree with Dimitra's decision? Why or why not?

_____

_____

_____

5. How were Shirley's attitudes destructive?

_____

_____

6. How were Felicia's attitudes constructive?

_____

_____

7. How could Shirley have been a better employee?

_____

_____

_____

8. Now that Shirley does not have a job, what advice would you give her before she starts looking for a new job?

_____

_____

_____

_____

Analyze

No matter how negatively you feel about others, do not let it show in the workplace. You might have to smile when you don't feel like it. You might have to swallow your pride or your anger. In the world of work, bad attitudes are destructive; and the thing that will be destroyed is your chance for success.

Compare Negative and Positive Attitudes

Shirley was an efficient server. However, her negative attitude was destructive. It caused problems in her relationship with José. It caused customers to not return. Felicia was less efficient than Shirley, but her constructive attitude encouraged customers to return. Dimitra could see this, and Felicia is the one who kept her job.

Today, most jobs are in the service industry. The service industry consists of businesses that provide a service, such as restaurants, hotels, airlines, salons, mass transportation, and medical care. A major part of many service jobs is interaction with customers. To be successful in your job and for your organization to be successful (so that you can stay employed), your interactions with customers must be positive.

Even when customer interactions are not direct, employees in service organizations have an impact on customers. For example, if you work in the kitchen of a restaurant as a chef or support staff to a chef, you don't serve the customers, but customers will not return if they don't like the food. The same is true of office workers, warehouse workers, and transportation workers who make service operations run successfully behind the scenes. The service industry needs people who combine high productivity with a pleasant, positive attitude like Felicia's.

Prejudice and Discrimination

Shirley might be surprised to be labeled a bigot, but her attitude indicates that she is. A bigot is a person who lacks tolerance for others who are different from them in some way. This lack of tolerance is usually based on negative beliefs about groups of people. Shirley's negative attitude toward José was based on negative beliefs about immigrants.

Prejudice is hostility toward a group of people. Prejudice is usually based on external characteristics, such as race, gender, or age. A set of beliefs, often based on generalizations that are false, are then developed for that group of people. Racism is prejudice based on race or ethnicity. Ageism is prejudice based on age. Sexism is prejudice based on gender.

Prejudice is an obstacle to good human relations because it prevents people from seeing each person as an individual. Prejudice cuts off communication between people.

Shirley's racism has prevented her from seeing José as a productive member of the team. Unlike Felicia, she does not see him as an individual, but as one of "those people." Not only has her attitude interfered with her developing a friendly relationship with José, but it has also interfered with her ability to work with him.

Shirley's ageism prevents her from seeing senior citizens as individuals deserving of her attention. Instead, she looks at her elderly customers as part of a bothersome group.

Sexism negatively influences relationships among employees, supervisors, and customers. An example of sexism is wrongly assuming a person cannot do a job simply because of their gender identity.

Prejudice can be responsible for seemingly minor destructive actions like impatience or abruptness. Unchecked, it can lead to arrogance or outright rudeness in dealings with others. Prejudice can also be the basis of actions that favor others as well as cause harm. A person may underestimate or overestimate the abilities of others because of their attitude about gender or gender identity, race, ethnicity, age, or sexual orientation.

Discrimination is the term for negative actions targeted at individuals based on their race, nationality, religion, gender, or sexual orientation. Laws protect employees from discrimination in the workplace. These same laws protect customers from discrimination by employees. As an employee, you represent the business, not yourself. Therefore, you are responsible for treating everyone with equal respect and courtesy. Treating everyone with respect is easy to do when you have a positive attitude and practice good human relations.

Oversensitivity

Being overly sensitive is another destructive attitude that can limit your effectiveness. Oversensitivity means taking slights and mistakes too personally or seriously. Small incidents may become major upsets. The overly sensitive worker may spend too much time nursing wounded feelings. Meanwhile, work goes undone.

Selfishness

Selfishness is a trait of people who have the attitude that their needs and concerns are more important than those of others. In the workplace, they may tend to put their own interests first, without being concerned for the effect on their coworkers. A team member may be late with their tasks on a project and expect the other members to be patient or pick up the slack. Selfish people expect others to cater to their needs without feeling compelled to return the favor. Because they are primarily concerned with themselves, they are often lacking in self-awareness in their dealings with others.

Dissatisfaction

Dissatisfaction is the state of being unhappy and seeing the negative side of things. A coworker with a destructive attitude can take the joy out of a job for you and those who work with you. Nothing is right or good for the dissatisfied worker. The boss is a jerk, the hours are bad, the raise was too small, and the customers are rude. One dissatisfied worker can spread negativity like a disease and reduce everyone's productivity.

For some people, always looking for the negative becomes a full-time occupation. Beware of dissatisfied coworkers. Do not let them change your positive attitude to a negative one. The energy you spend dwelling on the negatives can be put to better use.

Counteract Destructive Attitudes

Destructive attitudes affect everything you do. They have a negative effect on your relationships with supervisors, coworkers, and customers. One way to avoid negative attitudes is to become aware of them.

To counteract destructive attitudes, study your responses to others. Because attitudes are often unconscious, you may not be aware of your destructive responses. To help you become more self-aware, ask yourself the following questions:

- Do I have negative attitudes about a group of people?
- How do I respond to someone who is different from me?
- Do I get angry or behave rudely to people for no obvious reason?
- Am I oversensitive about certain matters?
- Do I behave selfishly toward others?
- Do I expend too much energy on feeling dissatisfied or negative?

By honestly answering these questions, you might become aware of unconscious prejudices or selfish feelings that may be based on past experiences or attitudes formed over time. Take the opportunity to examine your answers and make adjustments if needed.

Drazen Zigic/Shutterstock.com

MBI/Shutterstock.com

Apply

Case: Mary and the Malcontents

Mary works in the shoe department of a large department store. She uses a tablet to enter the customer's requested styles into the stockroom system, and then must make a trip downstairs to pick up the stock. Sometimes there is a line of salespersons waiting for their customers' requests. On busy days, customers often become angry when it takes her a long time to return with the shoes they want.

Mary is unhappy because the customers are dissatisfied. She tries not to lose patience, but when a customer blames her for taking so long, she speaks up. She explains that she is doing the best she can; it is the store's system that is at fault. Sometimes customers leave before she returns with their shoes, so she has started telling customers that it will take a while to get their size or color. She often adds that if they don't want to wait, they can just say so and not waste her time.

Some customers have complained to Mary's supervisor, and she is worried that she might lose her job if more complaints are received. She finds it hard to understand why her future depends on the opinions of people who shouldn't be shopping if they don't have the time. Since the store's system is the reason customers are unhappy, why is she being blamed?

Case Analysis

1. List three options for dealing with Mary's job situation.

_____
_____
_____
_____
_____
_____

2. List the option you would choose, and explain why you would choose it.

_____
_____
_____
_____
_____
_____
_____
_____
_____

Review

True or False

Indicate *T* if the statement is true or *F* if the statement is false.

1. _____ When workers are productive, they can get away with negative attitudes.

2. _____ Racism is a form of prejudice that is based on membership in a particular racial or ethnic group.

3. _____ Racism, ageism, and sexism are three examples of constructive attitudes.

4. _____ Prejudices are based on true generalizations about groups of people.

5. _____ Destructive attitudes cut off communication between people.

6. _____ Oversensitivity means being very sensitive to the needs of others.

7. _____ Selfish workers are often tactless and inconsiderate in their relationships.

8. _____ One dissatisfied worker can spread a negative attitude and reduce group productivity.

9. _____ A person cannot do anything to change a destructive attitude.

10. _____ People are usually aware of their negative attitudes and the destructive consequences that could result.

Check Your Understanding

1. What is a destructive attitude?

_____

_____

_____

_____

_____

2. Why do jobs in the service industry require constructive attitudes?

_____

_____

_____

_____

_____

3. Give an example of how a destructive attitude can cause problems on the job.

_____

_____

_____

_____

_____

4. Name six types of destructive attitudes.

_____

_____

_____

_____

5. Describe a destructive attitude. What can you do to counteract it?

_____

_____

_____

_____

Journal Writing

1. Think about a destructive attitude of yours or a peer's. What impact has it had on your job or studies?

_____
_____
_____
_____
_____
_____
_____
_____
_____
_____
_____
_____
_____
_____

2. Answer these questions: Do I get angry or rude to people for no obvious reason? Am I oversensitive about certain matters? Am I dissatisfied or negative about anything? If you answered yes to any of these questions, use your journal to explore your answers. Write why you get angry, are oversensitive, or are negative. Write about ways you could lessen or resolve your anger, oversensitivity, or negativity.

_____
_____
_____
_____
_____
_____
_____
_____
_____
_____
_____
_____

Are Your Attitudes Destructive?

Which of the following words describe your attitude? For each word, rate yourself on the following scale:

5 = always, 4 = often, 3 = sometimes, 2 = rarely, 1 = never

Then, go back through the list. If the word describes a constructive attitude, put your rating in the "Constructive" column. If the word describes a destructive attitude, put your rating in the "Destructive" column. There are five constructive words and five destructive words.

Attitudes	Your Rating	Constructive	Destructive
accepting			
angry			
dissatisfied			
helpful			
loyal			
oversensitive			
polite			
prejudiced			
selfish			
sincere			
Totals	Total Ratings:	Total:	Total:

Scoring

Add the ratings for the words in the Constructive column.

My score for constructive attitude is _____.

Add the ratings for the words in the Destructive column.

My score for destructive attitude is _____.

Now subtract your destructive score from your constructive score.
(Constructive score – Destructive score = Final score)

My final score is _____.

Interpretation

Score	Meaning
25	Perfect score! You have a great attitude!
15 to 24	Your attitude is good.
0 to 14	Your attitude is okay, but could be much better.
Less than 0	Your attitude is mostly destructive and could be interfering with your chance of success.

Action

It is always a good idea to work on improving your attitude; but the lower your score, the more work you need to do. Below, list the problem areas you need to work on. For each problem area, describe one way to improve. Focus on one area for at least a week. When you have improved in that area, work on another. Continue until you think you have improved in all your problem areas. If your score is 14 or lower, you might want to meet with a trusted person who knows you well to discuss ways to improve your attitude.

Ways to Change My Destructive Attitudes

_____
_____
_____
_____
_____
_____
_____
_____
_____
_____
_____
_____
_____
_____
_____
_____
_____
_____
_____
_____
_____
_____
_____
_____
_____
_____
_____
_____
_____
_____
_____
_____
_____
_____
_____

7 Constructive Attitudes

Objectives

- Define a constructive attitude.
- Explain the difference between a positive attitude and a constructive attitude.
- Explain what it means to be proactive.

Key Terms

constructive attitude

proactive

goodwill

Odua Images/Shutterstock.com

A constructive attitude combines being positive with taking action to get results.

Case

Employee of the Month

Jada and Tia are salespeople in the sports equipment and clothing department of a local clothing store. They are both good workers and enjoy their jobs. They stay informed about fashion and sports trends and attend workshops offered by the various manufacturers.

The store is finding it hard to maintain profits with the growing number of online shoppers. The owner, Mariko, calls the staff together for a meeting. She tells them, "You're all doing a great job, but we need to increase sales. I'm asking you to make the most of the summer season and push harder on sale items and repeat customers.

"We are going to start an award for Employee of the Month. The winner will be the person who increases their monthly sales by the highest percentage. You will receive a $500 bonus and your picture will be displayed on our new Wall of Fame in the front of the store." The employees like the idea.

The store has many good employees. Since sales have been rising in the sports equipment and clothing department, Mariko has narrowed her choice to Jada or Tia. She watches as Jada greets customers on a busy Saturday.

"Hello, Mrs. Jamison, what can I do for you today? I bet you want another pair of those great golf shoes you bought last month, right?"

"Well, no, Jada. I actually came by just to pick up a supply of golf balls, but now that you mention it, I might give those shoes a thought."

"Well, you should, because they happen to be on sale right now. If you really like the fit and feel, think about getting two pairs. You never know; the styles might change next season."

Mrs. Jamison chuckles. "You drive a hard bargain, Jada. I don't know about two, but one backup pair on sale might be a good deal."

"Coming right up," Jada says with a smile. "While I get them, look around and take advantage of the rest of our sale items. Your size is right over here. I know you like these shirts."

Mariko smiles as she observes Mrs. Jamison leaving the store with two shopping bags—so much for just needing golf balls. Jada seems to know her customers. Most of the regulars go straight to her for help. In fact, when business is slow, there might be two or three regular customers waiting for Jada while Tia is not busy.

Tia is efficient and friendly. She smiles at a customer looking at the sale items, and says, "Let me know if you need help with sizes. We have more in the back." She then goes back to folding items and waits for the customer to approach her. She leaves customers alone to browse while she is refolding items and placing them neatly back on the tables. Meanwhile, Jada is taking a customer's order for an item that is out of stock and promising to call when it comes in. She helps customers find sale items and offers to place special orders. Mariko sees why sales are rising. Jada takes the extra steps to close the sale.

When the numbers come in, Mariko knows who her first employee of the month will be. Jada's sales have increased more than any other salesperson. She provides the extra service that closes sales and brings customers back. Mariko thinks Jada could teach others how to "close the sale." She asks Jada to offer a workshop on sales techniques to all the sales staff.

Case Analysis

After you have read the case *Employee of the Month*, answer the following questions.

1. Describe Jada's interaction with customers.

_____

_____

_____

2. Describe Tia's interaction with customers.

_____

_____

_____

3. What is the difference between Jada's and Tia's human relations skills?

_____

_____

_____

4. Jada and Tia approach their work differently. Is one right and the other wrong? Why?

_____

_____

_____

5. Which salesperson would you prefer? Why?

_____

_____

_____

6. What does this salesperson do to communicate her attitude to customers?

_____

_____

_____

7. Do you agree that the right person was chosen as Employee of the Month? Explain.

_____

_____

_____

Analyze

A friendly face is a good start, but a constructive attitude is more than that. A **constructive attitude** combines being positive with taking action to get results. Jada and Tia are equally positive, and both are good workers. Jada stood out because her constructive attitude made her a better salesperson. She used her human relations skills to develop trust with her customers. She showed an effort to look out for their interests by pointing out sales items and offering to take special orders. Jada also remembered her customer's preferences and past purchases and used that to her advantage to get more sales.

Mariko also showed a constructive attitude by giving employees incentive to increase sales and offering additional training to help everyone succeed.

This approach led to greater productivity. In today's job market, a constructive attitude is highly valued.

Action Is Key

People who have constructive attitudes are **proactive**. They take action to make changes or solve problems rather than reacting to things that happen. A salesperson searches the stockroom for a customer's preferred style and color. A building manager schedules regular inspections instead of waiting for things to break down. A project manager holds weekly team meetings to identify and head off problems that might cause delays.

Proactive people do not wait to be asked to do something. They recognize situations that have the potential to cause problems and work out ways to avoid them. They use their past experience and creativity to figure out more productive ways of doing things. If they finish a task early, they find additional tasks or ask their supervisor for more work.

A Constructive Attitude Creates Goodwill

People with constructive attitudes create goodwill. **Goodwill** is a positive feeling that occurs when someone does something that benefits you. A business wants to build goodwill among its customers and the community at large. One way to build goodwill is to develop a workforce that is well trained and enthusiastic about the organization's mission and goals.

Mariko used her awards program to identify the store's best workers. She publicly recognized Jada's skills and also gave her the opportunity to help her coworkers succeed. In this way, goodwill was created among the staff as well as the customers.

Jada created goodwill toward the store by her interactions with customers. She made them feel special and valued, and these good feelings encouraged them to return. In this way, workers with constructive attitudes help their companies succeed.

A Constructive Attitude Helps Workers Succeed

Supervisors appreciate workers with a constructive attitude. Such workers usually are more productive and more successful in their careers. Supervisors do not have to worry about proactive workers. Proactive workers will come to the supervisor when they see a problem brewing or need help.

A constructive attitude also helps when you have a bad day. Personal or work problems can interfere with your focus. It is hard to concentrate when you are worried about something. A constructive attitude helps you put aside your problems and remain actively involved in your work.

Jacob Lund/Shutterstock.com

Apply

Case: Handling a Bad Day

You have had a terrible morning. You spilled juice on yourself and had to change clothes. This made you late for work and, as you were settling down, a friend sent you a text canceling your weekend plans. As you start to work on a report due at the end of the day, your mother calls to tell you that your favorite uncle was rushed to the hospital with chest pains. Just then, your manager walks over to your desk to ask you to take on a new emergency job task. She wants to know if you can work on it right away because she needs it for a meeting at 10 o'clock.

Nutlegal Photographer/ Shutterstock.com

Case Analysis

1. List four options for responding to your manager.

_____

_____

_____

_____

_____

_____

_____

_____

_____

_____

_____

_____

2. List the option you would choose, and explain why you would choose it.

_____

_____

_____

_____

_____

_____

_____

_____

_____

_____

_____

_____

Review

True or False

Indicate *T* if the statement is true or *F* if the statement is false.

1. _____ A positive attitude is all that is needed to have good human relations.

2. _____ A constructive attitude means taking action to get results.

3. _____ To create goodwill with a customer, a salesperson must get them to make a purchase.

4. _____ Being able to put aside personal problems contributes to having a constructive attitude.

5. _____ Proactive workers never need help from others.

6. _____ It is easy to concentrate on work when you have personal worries.

7. _____ Waiting to be asked to do something is a trait of proactive people.

8. _____ Workers with constructive attitudes tend to create goodwill in their customers.

9. _____ Goodwill in the community is important to building relationships with customers.

10. _____ A constructive attitude can help workers cope with bad days.

Check Your Understanding

1. Explain the difference between a positive attitude and a constructive attitude.

   _____

   _____

   _____

   _____

   _____

   _____

   _____

   _____

2. How can a constructive attitude help you succeed at work?

   _____

   _____

   _____

   _____

   _____

   _____

   _____

   _____

3. What advice would you give Tia to help her have a constructive attitude?

   _____

   _____

   _____

   _____

   _____

   _____

   _____

   _____

4. Define goodwill.

   _____

   _____

   _____

   _____

   _____

   _____

   _____

Journal Writing

1. Recall a recent experience with someone who had a constructive attitude. Describe the attitude and the result of the person's behavior.

_____

_____

_____

_____

_____

_____

_____

_____

_____

_____

_____

_____

_____

_____

_____

_____

_____

2. Describe one of your constructive attitudes and how it helped you in your work, in a relationship, or at school.

_____

_____

_____

_____

_____

_____

_____

_____

_____

_____

_____

_____

_____

_____

_____

_____

_____

Developing Constructive Attitudes

It is hard to have a constructive attitude all the time. The goal is to respond to situations constructively as often as possible. Five situations are described below. For each one, give an example of how you responded (or could respond) with a constructive attitude and an example of a destructive response.

Situation	Constructive Response	Destructive Response
You are running late with your tasks on a team project.		
Your project is behind schedule because some of the team members cannot find the information they need.		
One of the new members of your department constantly interrupts you to ask questions.		
You are having trouble concentrating because two colleagues are chatting near your desk.		
An instructor gave you a lower grade than you expected, and you are upset.		

8 Morale

Objectives

- Define morale.
- Explain how high morale can lead to success at work.
- Explain how low morale can lead to problems at work.

Key Terms

morale
self-confidence
overqualified

Morale influences success at work.

mavo/Shutterstock.com

Case

The Perfect Job

Caitlin is the manager for a busy nail salon. She enjoys working with the owner and her coworkers. She likes the work, but has no interest in the salon business as a career. Caitlin's goal is to work with animals to decide if she wants to become a veterinarian.

One morning, Caitlin's dad notices an ad for a front desk manager at the local pet hospital. He says to Caitlin, "This sounds like the perfect job for you." Caitlin agrees and goes to the hospital that afternoon to apply for the job.

The interview goes very well, and Jessica, the business manager, offers Caitlin the job on the spot. Caitlin accepts and resigns from her job at the nail salon.

On her first day, Caitlin meets her coworker, Jovan. "You're lucky. The person who had your position is still here," says Jessica. "Jovan will train you and provide any help you need until you get adjusted."

Caitlin feels relieved because she was already a little worried. During her interview, she hadn't noticed how small and crowded the reception area is. Her desk is crammed into a tight corner and piled high with papers and files.

"This place is great," Jovan assures Caitlin. "I studied veterinary technology, and now I prepare instruments for surgery and help handle the animals during examinations."

Caitlin is excited about learning her new job. She loves to bring order to chaos, and the desk looks as if no one has done any filing in months. Each veterinarian has an appointment book, and she wonders why they don't use electronic calendars. "I'll fix that as soon as I get a chance to talk to Jovan about it," she says to herself. However, Jovan is always rushed, and they are constantly interrupted as he tries to explain things to Caitlin. She tries hard to make sense of Jovan's incomplete instructions, but it is difficult.

Pet owners and their pets come and go all day long. The activity is nonstop. Caitlin's plans to update the office systems sit on Jessica's desk for weeks. Jessica is always too busy or out of the office on business.

Caitlin loves seeing the pets and meeting their owners. However, because of the constant paperwork, there is barely time to say hello or pet the animals. All day, it's "sign this form, please." and "what method of payment, please?" She never gets a chance to talk to the veterinarians. They just nod and rush past her desk.

As time goes by, Caitlin feels more and more unhappy at work. She doesn't see any potential to learn more about the world of pet care. There is little interaction with her coworkers or with the pet owners and pets. Caitlin does not feel appreciated or part of a team.

After two months, Caitlin learns that her former job at the nail salon is available. She resigns her job at the pet hospital and returns to the nail salon.

Case Analysis

After you have read the case *The Perfect Job*, answer the following questions.

1. Describe Caitlin's attitude toward her job at the nail salon.

_____

_____

_____

2. Describe Caitlin's attitude toward her job at the pet hospital.

_____

_____

_____

3. What are the advantages and disadvantages of each job?

_____

_____

_____

4. Instead of quitting, what could Caitlin have done to improve her situation at the pet hospital?

_____

_____

_____

5. Describe Caitlin's morale at the nail salon.

_____

_____

6. Describe Caitlin's morale at the pet hospital.

_____

_____

_____

7. How did Caitlin's morale change after a few days on the job at the pet hospital?

_____

_____

_____

8. What would you have done in Caitlin's situation?

_____

_____

_____

Analyze

Morale refers to feelings and attitudes among employees about their work and the workplace. Managers are concerned about the morale of individuals in their work groups. They are also concerned about the morale of the work group as a whole.

High Morale Can Lead to Business Success

When morale is high, workers are confident. They enjoy their work and enthusiastically perform assigned tasks. The group feels unified and dedicated to reaching goals. A workplace where morale is high is a pleasant place to work. Employees are positive, and their high morale shows in their interactions with coworkers and customers. Workers perform better at their jobs, and customers are satisfied. High morale can lead to higher sales and business success.

Low Morale Can Lead to Poor Performance

When morale is low, the general attitude is negative. Workers dislike their work and are less willing to perform assigned tasks. The group does not care about goals or the future of the company. A workplace with low morale is an unpleasant place to work. Customers can tell if the morale of a business is low. The employees are likely to be rude and unhelpful. Low morale can lead to unhappy customers who do not return to the business.

Low morale can negatively affect job performance. If you are unhappy with your job responsibilities or your work environment, you may start to care less about your work. Why work hard if no one notices or appreciates you? If you receive only negative feedback from supervisors or coworkers, you may start to feel resentful. You may then dread going to work. A negative attitude may lead to being less careful about work, so performance may fall. Workers may be tempted to fake illness and skip work.

The Job Situation Affects Morale

Caitlin began her job at the pet hospital with high morale. She expected to like any job where she would be around animals. She assumed that her new coworkers would be like those on the job at the salon. Several factors led her morale to fall as time went on.

One of these factors was the workspace. Crowded and cramped, the space was small and poorly organized. Caitlin was used to working in more spacious surroundings. The lack of good training procedures was another factor. It was hard for Caitlin to know how to do her job when she lacked information. She was drowning in paperwork because no one had taken the time to install modern technology that makes record keeping more efficient.

Caitlin's coworkers were another factor in her low morale. The business manager and the veterinarians were too busy to teach her anything about the business. Her coworkers were also distant, adding to Caitlin's feeling that she was not part of a team. She no longer looked forward to going to work.

Your Confidence Affects Your Morale

How you feel about yourself influences your level of self-confidence. Having self-confidence means you feel sure of yourself and are secure in your ability to handle challenges or succeed at something. Some people have a strong sense of confidence in almost any situation. Others may feel more or less confident, depending on the circumstances.

When starting a new job, your level of confidence may waver at first. If you fear that you are not up to the challenge of the job, it may cause your morale to drop. Once you prove to yourself that you are capable of handling the new responsibilities, your morale is likely to rise again. If you receive positive feedback from others, your morale and confidence will get a boost. If you do not receive feedback, check in with your manager or coworkers to ask how you are doing.

Find Out the Cause of Low Morale

Caitlin started with high morale, but was soon unhappy. It is common to experience changes in your level of morale at work. Sometimes this happens from day to day. Sometimes your morale changes over a long period of time. As your goals change, your satisfaction level with your job may change.

Caitlin decided to leave the job she enjoyed at the nail salon because she wanted to pursue her goal of working with animals. If she had stayed longer with the hospital, she might have been able to help the office run more smoothly. The staff and management might have grown to appreciate her help and doors to her future career might have opened. In Caitlin's case, low morale caused her to give up before she gave the job a chance.

If you have long periods of low morale, you need to discover why. Ask yourself these questions:

- **Are you and the job a good fit? Are you doing what you want to do?** Caitlin enjoyed working with people. She liked to feel needed. One reason for her unhappiness and low morale at the pet hospital was that her contacts with patients were so limited. She missed being able to help her customers and coworkers as she did in the nail salon.

- **Are your expectations too high?** You may feel that you are not progressing fast enough. You may have expected to receive a promotion or raise that did not materialize. It might help to reevaluate your expectations and see if they are realistic. Caitlin expected to feel as comfortable at the pet hospital as she did at the salon. She assumed she would be welcomed and treated as a member of the team right away. Was this unrealistic?
- **Are you overqualified for your job?** Being overqualified means you have more knowledge and skills than a job requires. If your work is not challenging enough, your morale might fall. You might get very bored. You might feel disappointed in yourself or feel that your talents and skills are not being recognized. For this very reason, few employers will hire someone who seems overqualified for a job.

Quitting Is a Last Resort

Quitting should not be your first answer to low morale. There are often many things you can do to improve the situation.

In Caitlin's situation, should she have given it more time? Could she have talked to her supervisor about her concerns? How do you react when your expectations are not met? Speaking up and making constructive suggestions can improve things. Staying quiet and leaving a job is not always the answer.

If Caitlin had remained at the pet hospital, she might have helped improve the office morale. She could have shared with Jessica some ideas for making the office run more smoothly.

Discuss Low Morale with Your Supervisor

If you are struggling with low morale, talk to your supervisor. Do not focus on a laundry list of complaints about management or personal attacks on your coworkers. Keep the focus of the conversation on concrete problems that can be solved.

Before having the conversation, make a list. For each problem, develop a solution. For example, Caitlin had trouble keeping up with the patients because the files were so disorganized. She had ideas for improvement but felt no one took the time to listen to her. She made a list of her suggestions and left it on Jessica's desk, but Jessica was too busy to read it. Caitlin might have asked Jessica to meet with her early or late in the day when it was less busy. She might have offered to work overtime just to organize the files.

Before giving in to low morale, make it clear that you want to make things work better for the group and for the business. Once you have given it your best effort, you will feel better if leaving is the option you choose.

fizkes/Shutterstock.com

Apply

Case: Job Insecurity

Your company is in financial trouble. Several people have been laid off, and there are more layoffs coming. Your supervisor has told you that your job is secure; but with so many people being let go, it is hard to believe. Going to work is becoming more depressing every day. Coworkers have stopped working; instead, they are discussing the latest layoff or debating the company's future. You thought you would be able to advance your career at this company. Now you wonder what the future holds for your employer. In spite of the turmoil, you work hard at staying upbeat.

Case Analysis

1. List three options for dealing with your job situation.

_____

_____

_____

_____

_____

_____

_____

_____

_____

_____

_____

2. List the option you would choose, and explain why you would choose it.

_____

_____

_____

_____

_____

_____

_____

_____

_____

_____

_____

_____

Review

True or False

Indicate *T* if the statement is true or *F* if the statement is false.

1. _____ Morale refers to how productive a person is at work.
2. _____ A workplace where morale is high is nearly always a pleasant place to work.
3. _____ High morale has no impact on business success.
4. _____ Generally, workers are unaware of worker morale at a business.
5. _____ A lack of confidence can lead to low morale.
6. _____ A person's morale is affected only by the individual's own attitude, and the attitude of the work group has no effect.
7. _____ A cramped workspace causes low morale.
8. _____ Lack of confidence can lead to low morale.
9. _____ Discussing problems with your supervisor is a good way to improve low morale.
10. _____ Quitting is only one solution for problems at work.

Check Your Understanding

1. Describe a person with high morale.

_____

_____

_____

_____

_____

_____

_____

_____

2. Describe a person with low morale.

_____

_____

_____

_____

_____

_____

_____

_____

3. Explain how low morale in a work group can lower sales.

_____

_____

_____

_____

_____

_____

_____

_____

4. Describe two ways to handle low morale.

_____

_____

_____

_____

_____

_____

_____

_____

Journal Writing

1. Recall a situation, either in school or on a job, when your morale has been low. How did your low morale affect your productivity and your happiness?

_____

_____

_____

_____

_____

_____

_____

_____

_____

_____

_____

_____

_____

_____

_____

2. Self-confidence is an important element of morale. How self-confident are you? What raises or lowers your feelings of self-confidence? What could you do to improve your self-confidence?

_____

_____

_____

_____

_____

_____

_____

_____

_____

_____

_____

_____

_____

_____

9 Handling Stress on the Job

Objectives

- Describe the role of attitudes in lowering levels of stress.
- Explain the relationship between stress and aggression.
- List positive ways to deal with stress.

Key Terms

stress
stressors
aggressive behavior
verbal aggression
negative reinforcement

Stress is a normal part of life.

Liderina/Shutterstock.com

Case

The Stressed-out Supervisor

"I think I should just quit," says Juan. "I can't do anything right!"

"Juan, that's not true," his manager, Susan, responds. "All I asked was that you be more careful when you proofread. The last promotional e-mail had misspellings. Errors hurt sales."

"I quit," Juan replies. "I do a good job with a small staff. If I slip up once in a while and a small error gets through, the whole department looks bad. It's a no-win situation for me."

"Now, don't do anything hasty," Susan cautions. "You worked hard for your promotion. You've been a supervisor for only a short time, and you have been doing well. Don't let one little criticism stop you. It is part of the job."

"Sure, it goes with the job," Juan agrees. "I just don't know if being a supervisor is for me."

"Why, Juan? You're doing a good job and you're paid well for what you do," Susan reminds him.

"I know I make a lot more than I did before the promotion, but then I didn't take the job home with me. Now it's on my mind all the time. I worried all last night about the mailings I approved yesterday. I rechecked them this morning, and they are okay; but that didn't give me back the lost sleep."

"Quitting is not the answer, Juan," Susan explains. "You have to learn how to handle stress. There is going to be some stress in every job."

"What do you suggest I do?" Juan asks.

"First," Susan says, "Take a look at how you're scheduling work. What methods are you using to maintain quality and meet deadlines?"

"I make a schedule for the tasks I must accomplish. I keep track of each task and its due date. If I get off track, I analyze the situation to determine how to get back on track. It's just that sometimes the workload is bigger than I can handle."

"When that happens, come to me. Until we get more staff, I'll try to help you by slowing down the number of mailings we're putting out. Look for constructive ways to keep control of things during the day. I don't want you losing sleep anymore. That certainly won't help your morale."

"You're right. I have been feeling worn out for the past few weeks."

"I'll tell you what I do. I eat healthy foods, exercise, and get eight hours of sleep. When I'm away from work, I don't think about it. I focus on quality time with family and friends. When I return to work, I feel refreshed and can concentrate fully. When you relax and enjoy life outside of work, you will be able to cope better with stress on the job."

Juan listens thoughtfully. "Thanks, Susan. I appreciate your understanding and advice. I will try your suggestions, and I'm not going anywhere until I do." Juan leaves with a smile on his face for the first time in weeks.

Case Analysis

After you have read the case *The Stressed-out Supervisor,* answer the following questions.

1. What triggered Juan's frustration?

_____

_____

_____

2. What was Juan's attitude toward handling problems on the job?

_____

_____

_____

3. What was Susan's attitude toward her job?

_____

_____

_____

4. What was the main cause of Juan's initial decision to quit?

_____

_____

_____

5. Describe Susan's response to the problem.

_____

_____

_____

6. What was causing Juan's stress?

_____

_____

_____

7. List two other ways that Juan could have handled his stress.

_____

_____

_____

_____

Analyze

Stress is a feeling of general anxiety, mental tension, or emotional distress. It has a variety of causes that stem from personal circumstances to very demanding situations at work. These causes of stress are called stressors, and they are different for each individual. Get to know what your stressors are so that you can find ways to avoid them or work around them.

Do you hate to get up in the morning? When you are running late and get stuck in traffic, you feel general stress. Do you procrastinate? When you are trying to finish the term paper due tomorrow morning, you feel mental stress. Do you have problems in your relationships? When you have an argument with someone, you feel emotional stress.

There are ways to avoid stress. You can make a habit of leaving earlier for appointments and starting your papers further in advance. You can avoid confronting issues with coworkers, supervisors, friends, and loved ones. However, there is no way to avoid *all* stress. Stress is an inevitable part of life. In fact, some stress is actually good for you. Stress can motivate you to confront a problem and take action to find a solution.

Stress Is Related to Destructive Attitudes

Stress at work may be the cause of a destructive attitude or it may be the result of it. Juan's attitude toward his job was destructive. His career was progressing well, but he was willing to give up his success to avoid stress. His stress was caused by taking on new responsibilities and having to meet high standards based on other people's work. Instead of being constructive in finding a solution for his problem, he allowed himself to become negative. His destructive attitude caused him to want to give up and quit.

If you approach your job with destructive attitudes, you will limit your opportunity for growth. Every job has problems; thinking about quitting is not the solution to problems on the job. Juan made a wise choice by talking over his feelings with Susan. She gave him good advice that might help him turn things around. Developing constructive attitudes will help you find solutions and eliminate stress.

Find Ways to Handle Stress

Stress is a normal part of life. It does not just go away. You need to find ways to handle situations that cause you stress. If you do not handle your stress, it can build up. The buildup of stress can negatively affect your performance, your attitude, and even your health.

How you deal with stress on the job can affect your career positively or negatively. Even in a job you love, you will experience stress at some point. There are acceptable and unacceptable ways to deal with stress.

Unacceptable Ways to Relieve Stress

Stress can cause feelings of anger and frustration. It can be tempting to act out these feelings by aggressive behavior. **Aggressive behavior** involves actions that are hostile or destructive, such as yelling, walking out, slamming doors, or threatening someone. When you react to stress with aggressive behavior, you are taking out your negative feelings on others and doing nothing to solve the problem. In fact, you are probably making it worse. Aggressive behavior is unacceptable at work. It is often grounds for being fired immediately.

Verbal aggression can also cause problems at work. **Verbal aggression** is speaking in a hostile or angry way. Juan's verbal aggression was his threat to quit. Threats to quit might make you feel better; however, they serve no constructive purpose. The cause of your stress is still there. Also, if you threaten to quit, your boss might just respond, "That's fine with me. Your resignation is accepted."

Juan let his stress build to the point where he couldn't sleep. Then, when his manager made a reasonable request, he reacted angrily. He could have seriously damaged his relationship with Susan. Luckily, she understood Juan's anger and was sympathetic. However, now she may worry about his ability to handle increased responsibilities. Unless Juan is able to change, it is doubtful that he will get another promotion. In fact, Susan might decide to take away his management responsibilities if his stress continues.

Sometimes, you may find yourself on the receiving end of anger or aggression from supervisors, coworkers, or customers. While these actions will cause you stress, try to understand the cause and react calmly. Whenever someone speaks angrily to you, do not respond with anger. Angry arguments can damage relationships. Respond calmly to the person. If that does not lower their aggression, the best thing to do is to say that you will talk to them later.

Acceptable Ways to Relieve Stress

When you feel your stress level rising, try to relieve it in an acceptable way. It is a good idea to seek the advice of a person who is not involved in the situation. However, be wise about your choice of coworkers. Venting stress to the wrong person can backfire. It might be best to choose someone outside the workplace if you feel the need to vent about your boss, your coworkers, or your company. Words spoken in anger or to the wrong person can come back to haunt you.

Talk with Someone You Trust

Talking with someone you trust can give you insight into your situation. Sometimes, just the act of talking is enough. Expressing your feelings relieves stress and may help you focus more on solutions.

If you know someone who has experience in the workplace, ask for suggestions on ways to handle your situation. A friend or family member might be able to help you see things more clearly. Make sure the person you confide in is someone with a positive attitude. The last thing you need is negative reinforcement. Negative reinforcement is encouragement of negative attitudes, such as when you talk with someone who encourages your negative feelings.

Become Physically Active

Maintaining a constructive attitude when stressed will be easier if you have an outlet for your negative feelings. Physical activity is an excellent way to discharge stress. Walk, run, bicycle, swim, dance, or do some cleaning. At work, do something physical if you possibly can. Shred old paperwork, or use your lunchtime to take a brisk walk.

Analyze Your Feelings

If talking does not help, try analyzing the situation in writing. Reading what you have written about your feelings can help you see them more objectively. Are your feelings justified, or are you being too sensitive? Are you blaming others or taking responsibility? You might also write about several ways to resolve the problem. Seeing the options in black and white may help you make a good choice.

Avoid Writing to Others

It is generally not advisable to send written communication when you are stressed or angry about a work problem. Angry spoken words may be forgotten. Angry written words will be around long after the situation that prompted them is over. They can be shared with others and cause the problem to escalate. If you write an angry e-mail to a coworker, rather than responding in kind, they might forward it to your manager. Such communications are very hard to explain and may permanently damage others' opinions of you.

If you receive angry or threatening messages from someone at work, you should seek help from the appropriate person.

Put Work in Its Place

Dealing with stress at work is easier if you have a balanced life. Family, friends, and outside interests can help you deal with stress. These outside activities will help you put work in perspective as one part of your life. Friends might confide in you about their stressors. Sometimes just hearing about the problems of others makes you see that yours aren't so terrible after all.

Doing activities you like will reinforce your positive feelings and help you approach your job with a constructive attitude. Spending time with people whose company you enjoy and helping others are constructive ways to relieve stress.

Apply

Case: The Delayed Promotion

You are transferred to a new department. You do not want to accept the transfer because you will have to work evening hours. You are assured that by accepting the transfer, you will make progress toward a supervisory position. You accept the transfer, and your manager is pleased with your work. After a year on the job, two of your coworkers in your previous department have been promoted. You feel that your move has not paid off. Your department budget has been cut back, and your workload has increased. You feel you deserve a promotion as promised. You tell your supervisor that you were led to believe you would be promoted when you took the transfer. Your supervisor tells you to be patient; it will happen soon. The next month, a coworker receives the promotion instead. You are furious.

Case Analysis

1. List three options for dealing with your job situation.

_____
_____
_____
_____
_____
_____
_____
_____
_____
_____

2. List the option you would choose, and explain why you would choose it.

_____
_____
_____
_____
_____
_____
_____
_____
_____
_____
_____

Review

True or False

Indicate *T* if the statement is true or *F* if the statement is false.

1. _____ Every job involves some degree of stress.
2. _____ Stress can be the cause of a destructive attitude.
3. _____ Aggressive behavior is one acceptable way of dealing with stress.
4. _____ Ignoring stress is the best thing to do.
5. _____ Verbal aggression is a good way to handle stress.
6. _____ Talking with a trusted person outside the workplace can give you insights into how to handle stress.
7. _____ Physical activity helps discharge negative feelings.
8. _____ Slamming doors and drawers at work will help discharge stress in a positive way.
9. _____ Writing an e-mail to the boss or a coworker when you are angry is never a good idea.
10. _____ An angry response is an appropriate response to verbal aggression.

Check Your Understanding

1. Describe a situation that could cause stress.

_____

_____

_____

_____

_____

_____

_____

_____

2. Describe two unacceptable responses to stress.

_____

_____

_____

_____

_____

_____

_____

_____

3. Describe two acceptable responses to stress.

_____

_____

_____

_____

_____

_____

_____

4. How can a balanced life help you deal with stress?

_____

_____

_____

_____

_____

_____

_____

Journal Writing

Write about a situation that is causing you stress. What is causing the stress? What are you doing to reduce the stress? If your reaction is destructive, how could you make your reaction constructive? If you are not doing anything, what can you do to try to reduce the stress?

_____

_____

_____

_____

_____

_____

_____

_____

_____

_____

_____

_____

_____

_____

_____

_____

_____

_____

_____

_____

_____

_____

_____

_____

_____

_____

_____

_____

_____

How Do You Handle Stress?

Everyone experiences stress at some time, and the best way to handle stress varies with the situation. This quiz can give you some insight into the way you cope with stress. Below is a list of ways a person might handle stress. Read each reaction. If the reaction is positive, place an X in the "Positive" column. If the reaction is negative, place an X in the "Negative" column. Then indicate each reaction that you have experienced.

Reaction to Stress	Positive	Negative	My Reactions
Blame others.			
Blame yourself.			
Clean up or organize.			
Clench your fists.			
Complain, complain, complain.			
Confide in a trusted friend.			
Count to ten silently.			
Daydream about your ideal job (or another situation).			
Eat candy or something else unhealthy.			
Give in to feeling depressed.			
Give others the silent treatment.			
Go out for a walk.			
Plan your revenge.			
Send a nasty e-mail, text, or post on social media.			
Slam a door.			
Swear under your breath.			
Tackle a task you have been avoiding.			
Take a coffee break.			
Talk about your problem so everyone can hear.			
Threaten to quit.			

Scoring

1. Count the number of positive reactions you chose. My positive score is _____.
2. Count the number of negative reactions you chose. My negative score is _____.

Interpretation

Even though many negative reactions are common, any of them can cause problems at work or personally. Your goal should be to change as many negative responses as possible to positive responses.

Action

Choose three of your negative reactions. If you did not have any negative reactions, choose three from the list, and give a suggestion for a better way to react.

1. Negative Reaction 1:

_____

A better way to react:

_____
_____
_____
_____
_____
_____
_____
_____

2. Negative Reaction 2:

_____

A better way to react:

_____
_____
_____
_____
_____
_____
_____
_____

3. Negative Reaction 3:

_____

A better way to react:

_____
_____
_____
_____
_____
_____
_____
_____

10   Rumors

Objectives

- Define the nature of rumors and the rumor mill.
- Describe the negative impact of rumors on the job.
- Explain the attitudes underlying development and passing of rumors.
- List ways to avoid the rumor mill.

Key Terms

rumor
misinformation
rumor mill
group mentality
confidential information
trade secrets
motive

The sharing of information can have positive or negative results.

Dean Drobot/Shutterstock.com

Case

The Rumor Mill

Marsha works for a luxury jewelry supplier. Yesterday, an important shipment was late in arriving to one of their major store customers. The customer was upset and threatened to find a new supplier. Marsha was asked to handle the problem.

Marsha had not been on the job for long. She was surprised to get such an important assignment. It was a challenge. She used all her customer relations skills to convince the customer to stay. The customer relations manager, Lee, was happy with her performance.

"Marsha," Lee says, "You did a wonderful job with saving that customer. They spend thousands of dollars with us every year. I had no doubt that you could handle it, though. I told the owner that you saved the account. If you keep up the good work, I expect that within six months you'll be promoted."

Marsha can hardly believe her ears. She tells her coworker Judith her good news.

"I'm happy for you, Marsha," Judith says, "but don't get your hopes up about that promotion. Lee's buddy, Kwame, told me he was sure he'd get that job. Everyone knows that Kwame is next in line. If you'd been here longer, you'd know that Lee often makes promises he doesn't keep."

Marsha feels completely deflated. Still, she resolves to do her best. As the months pass, she is given several major accounts. Lee often praises her performance.

Marsha's only regret is that the friendships she has formed at the office are changing. Judith occasionally asks her to lunch, but the lunches feel like cross-examinations. Judith is constantly pumping her for information.

A few months later, Lee announces Marsha's promotion to account manager. Several times that week, all conversation stops when Marsha enters the employee lounge. Marsha decides to ask Judith what the problem is.

"What am I doing wrong, Judith? Do people really resent me that much? I'm only doing the best job I know how. I didn't try to take this promotion away from Kwame. Do people think I badmouthed him? Is that the problem?"

Judith looks embarrassed. "Well, Marsha, maybe I shouldn't tell you this, but the rumor is that you and Lee are dating. That's why you've been promoted over Kwame. Everyone thinks Lee is playing favorites."

Marsha is shocked. "Judith, you know that's not true! Didn't you tell them the truth?"

Judith stammers, "What could I say? You told me yourself you had lunch with Lee, and he clearly likes you a lot."

"Are you kidding?!" Marsha exclaims. "We went across the street for a hot dog!"

"Well, he didn't ask anybody else to go. What other reason could there be for your quick promotion?"

Marsha is angry and confused. How did this happen?

Case Analysis

After you have read the case *The Rumor Mill*, answer the following questions.

1. What is your reaction to this case?

_____

_____

_____

2. What would you have advised Marsha to do about her coworkers' gossip?

_____

_____

3. What did Judith's behavior say about her attitude?

_____

_____

_____

4. What could Marsha have done to be proactive when she first heard the rumor?

_____

_____

_____

5. Describe Marsha's attitude toward her job.

_____

_____

6. Describe Judith's attitude toward her job.

_____

7. Do you think Lee did anything wrong? Explain.

_____

_____

_____

8. Describe another way that Judith might have responded to Marsha's news.

_____

_____

_____

Analyze

Communication plays a key role in all human relations. It is natural to share information with others. When you spend several hours a day with coworkers, you often talk with them about your personal life, your family, and work. You may talk about your joys and sorrows, successes and failures, hopes and fears. You also talk about information that you hear and the people with whom you work.

The sharing of information can have positive or negative results. Negative results occur when the information passed on is incomplete, wrong, or becomes exaggerated.

Rumors Usually Contain Misinformation

A rumor is widely spread information whose truth and source are unknown to the people who pass it around. Rumors often spread in places where the same group of people meet, such as a school or a workplace. Usually, the topic of the rumor is of great interest to the group of people. Because so many people are interested in the topics of rumors, they spread quickly.

Even if the information in a rumor is correct at the start, it usually changes along the way. Each time a new person hears the rumor and passes it on, the next person may change the content slightly. Usually this changing is not done on purpose. The new person may just add some thoughts or assumptions of their own. The rumor becomes misinformation, meaning it is untrue or incomplete information.

Rumors Are Spread by the Rumor Mill

How does information become misinformation? Worker A may overhear two supervisors talking about a possible layoff of one part-time worker. Worker A repeats this information to Worker B. Worker B then repeats it to Worker C. By the time Worker Z hears the information, its content has become "Major layoffs will occur in every department."

The process just described is called the rumor mill, also known as *gossip* in everyday life. Many people love gossip, but gossip is often untrue. Even if the information starts out true, it goes through the rumor mill and becomes misinformation.

Rumors Negatively Affect Productivity

When workers hear a rumor such as, "Major layoffs will occur in every department," they become alarmed. They become worried that their jobs may be cut. Productivity declines as workers spend time discussing the rumor. Workers lose their ability to concentrate on their work. This group mentality spreads until everyone has become less productive Group mentality is the tendency of the people in a group to think and behave in ways that conform.

Rumors Negatively Affect Relationships

Marsha's relationships with her coworkers were negatively affected by a rumor. They stopped talking to her and to each other in her presence. Marsha's happiness about her new promotion was spoiled by the rumor mill.

Rumors that involve company actions or events are bad enough, but rumors that damage coworkers personally are dangerous. Do not become a part of this kind of behavior in your workplace. It can lead to serious consequences that can hold you back. Vicious rumors that damage people's careers and reputations are taken seriously by managers and human resources departments. If formal complaints are made, the workers responsible may lose their own jobs or opportunities to advance.

How to Avoid the Rumor Mill

Marsha made a couple of mistakes. She shared Lee's positive comments with the wrong person. Judith felt loyal to Kwame. This loyalty may have affected her reaction to Marsha's news, or maybe Judith was jealous of Marsha's success. Either way, Judith couldn't wait to tell Kwame what Marsha had said. Kwame, who wanted the promotion for himself, was upset. His position as the next in line for promotion was threatened. The rumor mill began to make up reasons for Marsha's success.

Marsha also discovered that Judith was not trustworthy. You have probably had a similar experience. You told a secret to someone who could not wait to pass it on. After your secret was out, you regretted ever having talked about it. You became angry and upset with the "friend" whom you thought you could trust. At work, the best approach is simply this: if you do not want information to become common knowledge, do not share it with anyone. If you are on the receiving end of a rumor about work or hurtful information about someone, follow the tips below to avoid getting caught up in the rumor mill.

Avoid Negative Comments

Avoid negative comments about others. Negative talk, like a negative attitude, is destructive. If you hear something, keep it to yourself. When you talk to coworkers, assume that everything you say will be repeated. Do not say anything that would be embarrassing if people knew about it.

Rumors often start with negative comments about coworkers, supervisors, or the company's future. The rumor mill is especially active when companies undergo change; for example, when there is a reorganization or new ownership.

Be careful about "harmless rumors." Remember that what seems harmless can change in the retelling and become harmful. Examine your reasons for telling someone something, especially something negative. "If you can't say something nice, don't say anything" is old advice, but still true. Think of the rumors you have heard—how many were positive?

Do Not Share Confidential Information

Be especially careful about confidential information. Confidential information is private information intended for selected individuals. Many businesses have confidential information that people within the company must know, but which they do not want people outside the company to know. This type of information is also called trade secrets.

Confidential information can also be private personal information. People who work in parts of an organization that have access to employees' personal information, such as Social Security numbers or salaries, are trusted to respect that this information must be protected and kept private.

Employees who have access to confidential information as part of their job must take care to observe the privacy rights of individuals and the organization.

Do Not Believe Everything You Hear

When you hear negative comments, examine the motives of the person talking. A motive is the reason that explains a person's actions. When Judith warned Marsha not to get her hopes up about the promotion, what were her motives? Did she really want to warn Marsha of a problem? Maybe she was jealous and wanted to say something to make Marsha feel less confident. Maybe her loyalty to Kwame was leading her to say things that might discourage Marsha.

Marsha needed to examine Judith's comments about Lee in the same way. Judith appeared to be jealous of the recognition Marsha received from Lee. She wanted to put a damper on Marsha's motivation to go after the promotion. If Marsha had accepted what Judith said about Lee, the negative comments might have undermined Marsha's ability to work with Lee. If Marsha started having problems working with Lee, her performance might have fallen. It might have cost her the promotion.

Do Not Spread Rumors

Employees with constructive attitudes are less likely to spread rumors or spend time gossiping. Loyalty to an employer will also make workers less likely to repeat things that may not be true. Repeating negative information—or worse, making it up—is destructive behavior. When you hear negative information, gossip, or rumors, change the subject. Discuss a hobby, sports, or a movie.

MBI/Shutterstock.com

Apply

Case: New Manager, Many Rumors

You are happy with your job. You are good at what you do. The job is interesting and pays well, and you know what is expected of you every day. You worked well with your former manager, who left the company last month. You anticipate having the same good relationship with your new manager. However, you hear a rumor that the new manager plans to make sweeping changes in the organization of the department. You also hear that the new manager is a horrible person to work for. Coworkers are hinting that it's time to start looking for a new job.

Case Analysis

1. List three options for dealing with your job situation.

_____

_____

_____

_____

_____

_____

_____

_____

_____

2. List the option you would choose, and explain why you would choose it.

_____

_____

_____

_____

_____

_____

_____

_____

_____

_____

_____

_____

_____

Review

True or False

Indicate *T* if the statement is true or *F* if the statement is false.

1. _____ The sharing of information is always constructive.

2. _____ Rumors tend to spread in places where the same people get together every day.

3. _____ Rumors are good because they keep employees informed of management decisions.

4. _____ One rumor can negatively affect a large group of people.

5. _____ Rumors may start out fairly accurate, but may change completely as they are spread.

6. _____ People who spread rumors often have negative motives.

7. _____ Confidential information ceases to be confidential if shared with someone who should not receive it.

8. _____ Employees with constructive attitudes are most likely to start rumors because they communicate well with others.

9. _____ The rumor mill can make a good job more fun.

10. _____ Negative talk is as destructive as negative attitudes.

Check Your Understanding

1. What is a rumor?

_____

_____

_____

_____

_____

_____

_____

2. When correct information goes through the rumor mill, how does it become misinformation?

_____

_____

_____

_____

_____

_____

_____

_____

3. How can a rumor cause a decrease in productivity?

_____

_____

_____

_____

_____

_____

_____

_____

4. What can you do to avoid the rumor mill?

_____

_____

_____

_____

_____

_____

_____

_____

Journal Writing

Have you ever participated in a rumor mill? Describe the situation and how you participated. Did the rumor mill cause any harm or discomfort to anyone? Would you mind if the rumor mill spread rumors about you?

_____

_____

_____

_____

_____

_____

_____

_____

_____

_____

_____

_____

_____

_____

_____

_____

_____

_____

_____

_____

_____

_____

_____

_____

_____

_____

_____

_____

_____

_____

_____

_____

_____

_____

_____

_____

11   Accepting Responsibility

Objectives

- Explain the importance of accepting responsibility for your actions.
- Understand what to do when you make a mistake.

Key Terms

accepting responsibility
consequences

People who accept responsibility have a positive impact on those around them.

Marcos Castillo/Shutterstock.com

Copyright Goodheart-Willcox Co., Inc.

Case

Late Again

Amalie is an assistant in the editorial department of a magazine publishing company. Her work is good, and her boss likes her attitude. However, Amalie has trouble getting to work on time. On most days, she arrives a half-hour late, at 9:00 a.m. instead of 8:30 a.m. She says the reason is heavy traffic, and the bus she takes goes through construction.

Amalie frequently has difficulty getting started in the morning. She likes to stay up late. She often meets up with friends to eat out or binge watch their favorite shows. When she does not go out, she stays up late with friends on social media.

Shanice, Amalie's manager, must insist that Amalie arrive to work on time, but does not want to discourage her because her work is good. "It is not fair to the other employees," she explains. "They have already been working for a half hour by the time you get here."

Amalie has an idea. "What if I work half an hour later each day, with the understanding that I start half an hour later in the morning?"

"Are you sure that will make a difference? Will you be able to get here by 9:00 a.m. sharp?" Shanice asks. Amalie says yes. They agree to the new schedule.

For two weeks, Amalie is at work every day at 9:00 a.m. sharp. Gradually, however, she starts coming in later until she regularly arrives at 9:20 or 9:30. After another two weeks, Shanice talks with Amalie again. Amalie says, "I'm sorry. I really am trying. The traffic is even worse at the later hour. I think it will work better if I come in at 9:30 and leave at 5:30."

"Absolutely not," says Shanice. She points out that everyone must deal with traffic in the morning. "Since you could not make the special arrangement work, in fairness to everyone else, you must come in at 8:30." Shanice makes a note in Amalie's file to monitor her. She tells Amalie, "You may be put on probation if you continue to arrive late, and there will be no raises or promotion until you consistently arrive on time."

Case Analysis

After you have read the case *Late Again,* answer the following questions.

1. What is your reaction to this case?
_____
_____

2. Describe Amalie's attitude toward work.
_____
_____

3. Did Shanice help Amalie by allowing her to come in at a later time?
_____
_____

4. Describe what Amalie could have done to avoid the consequences of her lateness.
_____
_____

5. If you were Amalie's coworker, how would you feel about Amalie's change of hours?
_____
_____

6. Did Shanice take the right steps after Amalie continued to be late?
_____
_____
_____

7. What would you have done if you had been Amalie's supervisor?
_____
_____
_____

8. What advice would you give to Amalie?
_____
_____
_____

Analyze

Accepting responsibility is an important human relations skill.
Accepting responsibility means being willing to answer for your
actions and decisions. It also means being willing to accept the
consequences, the results of an action or behavior. People who accept
responsibility have a positive impact on those around them.
People who refuse to accept responsibility have a negative impact. At
work, this affects both relationships and group productivity.

Don't Blame Others

People who are unwilling or unable to accept responsibility for their
actions usually have poor human relations skills. They often try to blame
someone or something else. Here are some examples of not accepting
responsibility:

"I couldn't finish the report. People kept interrupting me."

"I didn't do the task right because you didn't explain it clearly."

"I would have done it better if you had let me do it my way."

"I don't know what happened to it. I just can't find it."

You can probably think of other examples. How do people who use
these excuses make you feel? Are you eager to work with them? People
who cannot take responsibility for their actions annoy their coworkers.
Soon, bigger problems may result, as happened in Amalie's case.

Solve the Problem

In a work setting, making excuses or blaming others is not acceptable. If
team members do not take responsibility for their mistakes or inaction,
how does that affect the team's success? Not taking responsibility may
result in work not being completed on time. Missing deadlines reduces
team productivity. The blaming does not solve the problem.

If you are unable to do your tasks on a project because a teammate
is holding up progress, don't sit back and wait for the deadline to slip. If
you don't consult with your teammate or your supervisor to try to solve
the problem, you are equally to blame for the delay.

Know Yourself

Accepting responsibility often requires a sound knowledge of yourself.
You need to be able to assess your own strengths and weaknesses.
Amalie blamed the traffic for her lateness. If she had looked at herself
honestly, she would have realized that she has a problem with getting up
in the morning. She was not accepting her responsibility to get to work
on time. She needs to solve this personal problem, not blame traffic.
Everyone deals with traffic, but only Amalie is always late to work.

Accepting responsibility does not mean that you have to accept blame or go around confessing. It does require you to know yourself. It requires that you think about what type of person you want to be and make adjustments to meet your goals. Amalie needs to find a way to get to work on time, or she will not be able to hold a normal office job.

If you cannot change your shortcomings, you will need to adjust your life accordingly. Amalie could explore jobs that start later in the day, although she might still have trouble getting to work then. A better solution would be to stop going out in the evenings during the workweek and get an earlier start in the morning.

Admit Mistakes and Correct Them

Accepting responsibility is closely related to another human relations skill: the ability to admit a mistake. It is easy to accept responsibility when things go well. The person with good human relations skills is able to accept responsibility when things go wrong. Doing so is good human relations because people respect and admire people who admit mistakes.

Acting responsibly is the first step toward correcting whatever the problem might be, but it is only a first step. You must follow through to correct the mistake or solve the problem. You must use all your human relations skills to work with your team and supervisor to prevent it from happening again.

michaeljung/Shutterstock.com

Apply

Case: The Unforeseeable Mistake

You are given an important report to complete and send to the company's printer by Friday. You are anxious to complete the report and get it off to be printed on Thursday because you have plans to take Friday off for vacation. Unfortunately, some information you need is delayed. By the time you get the information and finish the report, it is almost quitting time Thursday afternoon. Your coworker, Donald, says, "You go on and head home. I'll see to it that the report gets sent for printing tomorrow. How many copies do you need?" You gratefully accept the offer since the printing department cannot work on it before tomorrow anyway.

GaudiLab/Shutterstock.com

When you pick up the report from the printer on Monday, you are stunned to discover that it is printed in black ink, not colored ink. You left it to your coworker to fill out the print request instructions. It never occurred to you that such a mistake might occur. The meeting is this afternoon. There is no way the report can be reprinted on time. You are not looking forward to explaining the mistake to your boss.

Case Discussion

1. List three options for dealing with your job situation.

_____
_____
_____
_____
_____
_____
_____
_____
_____
_____

2. List the option you would choose, and explain why you would choose it.

_____
_____
_____
_____
_____
_____
_____
_____
_____
_____
_____

Review

True or False

Indicate *T* if the statement is true or *F* if the statement is false.

1. _____ When team members accept responsibility for their actions, the team is usually more productive.

2. _____ Being good at your job includes being able to accept the consequences of your actions.

3. _____ People who have an excuse for everything are failing to accept responsibility.

4. _____ Admitting a mistake is a serious error on the job.

5. _____ Accepting responsibility requires self-knowledge.

6. _____ Being responsible means it is acceptable to try to hide your mistakes.

7. _____ Accepting responsibility means confessing your weaknesses to others.

8. _____ If a worker has difficulty meeting a job's requirements, a solution might be to look for a more suitable job.

9. _____ Accepting responsibility when the consequences are negative is a constructive human relations skill.

10. _____ People look down on those who admit their mistakes.

Check Your Understanding

1. Explain how accepting responsibility for your actions is a human relations skill.

   _____
   _____
   _____
   _____
   _____
   _____
   _____
   _____

2. Give an example of accepting the consequences of an action that caused a mistake.

   _____
   _____
   _____
   _____
   _____
   _____
   _____
   _____

3. How can blaming others reduce team productivity?

   _____
   _____
   _____
   _____
   _____
   _____
   _____

4. Why is just admitting a mistake not enough?

   _____
   _____
   _____
   _____
   _____
   _____
   _____
   _____

Journal Writing

1. Give an example of a situation in which you made a mistake and accepted responsibility. How did others react to your willingness to accept responsibility?

_____

_____

_____

_____

_____

_____

_____

_____

2. Give an example of a situation in which you acknowledge that you did not accept responsibility. What was the result?

_____

_____

_____

_____

_____

_____

_____

_____

3. What could you have done to act more responsibly?

_____

_____

_____

_____

_____

_____

_____

_____

4. Describe a time when you were affected by someone who did not accept responsibility or did not act responsibly. How did you feel? What did you do?

_____

_____

_____

_____

_____

_____

_____

Taking Responsibility

Read the following statements. Which ones were made by a person who is accepting responsibility? Place an X in the Yes or No column for each statement. In the last column, write what you think the response of the supervisor or peers would be.

Responsible? Yes	Responsible? No	Statement	Response
		"You'd be late for work, too, if you had to take two buses every morning."	
		"Oh, no, we're out of paper. I should have ordered more last week."	
		"Nobody ever showed me the right way to do it. Am I supposed to be a mind reader?"	
		"I should have given you clearer directions."	
		"You promised to help me. It's your fault I missed the deadline."	
		"I thought I knew what to do. I'll work through lunch to fix this, and next time I'll ask for help sooner."	
		"She's a good teacher—I just didn't study enough for the exam."	
		"He distracted me. That's why I made the mistake."	

PART 3
Succeeding on the Job

Flamingo Images/Shutterstock.com

12 Communication

Objectives

- Understand how communication skills help you build positive relationships at work.
- Understand how nonverbal communication affects messages.
- Describe the attributes of being a good listener.
- Explain how a positive attitude helps you be an effective communicator.

Key Terms

communication
verbal communication
nonverbal communication
body language
active listening
miscommunication

Communication is the basis of good human relations.

GaudiLab/Shutterstock.com

Case

The Very Bad, Terrible, Horrible First Day

An insurance company has a small claims department that processes claims for more than 15,000 employees. The insurance claims adjusters process several forms for each claim. They must make sure payment checks are requested for doctors, hospitals, and labs. Every worker in the department has too much to do.

Raj arrives on Monday morning already feeling stressed. He had a backlog of past-due claims at the end of last week. On top of that, his supervisor has asked him to begin training Rachel, a new employee. Raj is sure this will be a terrible week.

Raj is deep into his work on a complicated claim when Rachel arrives. He looks up at her with a loud sigh. She says hello, and he gives her a brief nod. She sees that he seems annoyed at the interruption. He sits at his desk, stares at Rachel, and waits for her to talk. He taps his pencil impatiently.

Rachel, already anxious about the new job, fills the silence with nervous chatter about her previous job experience. Finally, Raj leans back in his chair, arms folded, and says, "I'm very busy today. I was asked to train you, and I will; but I don't want to know your life's history."

Rachel is embarrassed. When she arrived, she was sure of herself. She thought she would make a good first impression. Now Raj acts as if she is a nuisance. In a whisper, Rachel says, "I'm very sorry. I didn't mean to waste your time."

Raj looks down at his desk and moves some papers around without answering. He hands Rachel a writing pad and pen and proceeds to list her tasks. She writes very fast, but she can't keep up with his pace. He doesn't seem to notice. He jumps from topic to topic without stopping. When she interrupts to ask questions, his look tells her that she is brainless for not understanding. Rachel's self-confidence is fading.

Several times during the training session, the phone rings. Raj answers with a short "Yes?" and abruptly ends the calls. "At least," Rachel thinks, "it's not just me."

As the morning progresses, Rachel feels more and more lost. She tries to tell Raj, but he is not listening. He avoids eye contact with her.

At the beginning of her first day, Rachel was smiling. She was a bit nervous, but excited. She was looking forward to starting a new job and meeting new people. As she leaves at the end of the day, her shoulders are hunched and her head is down. The excitement is gone.

Case Analysis

After you have read the case *The Very Bad, Terrible, Horrible First Day*, answer the following questions.

1. Describe how Raj communicated verbally.

_____

_____

2. Describe how Raj communicated nonverbally.

_____

_____

3. What role did Raj's attitude play in his communication with Rachel?

_____

_____

4. What constructive action could Raj have taken to avoid being overloaded with work and training?

_____

_____

5. How would you rate Rachel's self-confidence on her first day on the job?

_____

_____

6. Give examples of how Rachel might have constructively responded to Raj's rudeness.

_____

_____

7. What role did Raj's attitude play in his communication with Rachel?

_____

_____

8. How did Rachel's body language show that her attitude had changed?

_____

_____

_____

9. Do you think Raj and Rachel can form a good working relationship after this first encounter? Why or why not?

_____

_____

_____

_____

Analyze

Communication is the process of sending messages from one person to another and receiving feedback. It is the basis of good human relations. Communication and attitude go hand in hand. The way you communicate sends messages about your attitude. Your attitude affects how you communicate. Both are keys to success in personal and work relationships. Productivity falls when workers cannot communicate and get along. The best product in the world may go unsold if the seller cannot communicate with the buyer. The most needed service may not be used if the attitude of the service provider is poor.

Communication skills are divided into two types: verbal communication and nonverbal communication.

Verbal Communication

Verbal communication consists of using words to send messages. Verbal communication includes speaking, writing, reading, and listening. Words provide us with a precise way to communicate a message. The clarity of the message depends on three things: your choice of words, your use of grammar, and how you organize your thoughts.

Your attitude can affect how well you choose your words and organize your thoughts. Raj was absorbed in his own problems. He had too much to do and had fallen behind. He felt negative about training Rachel. As a result, his choice of words conveyed his negative attitude: "I'm very busy today. I was asked to train you, and I will; but I don't want to know your life's history."

When it comes to your choice of words, make sure you leave any habit of using profanity or disrespectful language at the door when you enter the workplace. Even if others use such language, avoid being influenced by their behavior. Good manners and respect come across in how you speak.

Using correct grammar in speech and writing is also a good habit to practice at work. If you need to brush up on your grammar or spelling, use online resources for help or ask a coworker. Keep in mind that any flaws in how you speak or write might be overlooked in some workplaces, but practicing these positive habits will serve you well as you continue moving ahead in your career.

Nonverbal Communication

Nonverbal communication consists of everything you communicate *without* words. It includes hand gestures, facial expressions, posture, and position. Nonverbal communication is often called **body language**, but it also includes tone of voice and speed of speaking.

Raj's negative attitude was expressed in his body language, as well as his words. He avoided eye contact with Rachel, tapped his pencil, and spoke too fast. Such behaviors are even clearer than spoken words. Their message to Rachel was, "You annoy me, and I don't want to deal with you."

Being aware of your body language is key to good communication. Think about the simple act of not smiling when you meet someone. If the person is your friend, they might ask, "What's wrong?" If the person is a new acquaintance, they might think "not friendly" or "doesn't like me."

On the job, you have to be aware of what you are saying with your gestures, facial expressions, and tone of voice, as well as with your words.

Listening

Communication is a two-way street. Getting your message across is one part; using active listening skills is the other. Active listening means carefully listening to what is being said, observing nonverbal cues, and responding with appropriate feedback.

To do this, you need to hear what the other person is saying. When someone else is speaking, show that you are listening by making eye contact. Nod your head. Resist interrupting unless you do not understand what is being communicated. Hold up a hand if you want the person to stop so you can ask a question; or simply say, "Excuse me, I have a question." Letting someone go on and on when you don't understand might seem polite. However, leading someone to think you understand when you do not can cause problems.

Listening carefully and responding honestly are parts of being a good communicator. Be aware of the other person's nonverbal cues. If you are explaining something, notice if the person nods but also frowns. A frown can mean you are not being understood. You might need to stop and ask if there are any questions.

Active listening also means focusing on the speaker and not getting lost in thoughts of what you want to say. This is especially important when you have some area of disagreement. If you are too busy listening to your own thoughts, you cannot hear the other person. What happens when two people talk but do not really listen to each other? The result is miscommunication, which is a failure to communicate adequately and properly. Miscommunication often escalates into an argument.

Communication and Your Attitude

Raj's poor attitude toward training Rachel was evident through his verbal and nonverbal communication. Rachel felt a little better when she saw that Raj was rude to everyone. However, by the end of the day, Raj's negative attitude had affected Rachel. She no longer felt positive about her new job. If Raj's negative attitude continues, it will not inspire Rachel to work hard and do her best. If Raj were less stressed, he would welcome an eager worker who is willing to shoulder some of the overload.

Raj forgot that his job involved people as well as work tasks. He was asked to train a new person because he was good at his job. What will happen when his supervisor finds out Rachel did not learn very much on her first day? What will the supervisor think about Raj's ability to take on new job roles?

Much of your career success depends on how well you communicate. Good communication skills and good human relations skills go hand in hand. Your attitude influences the way you communicate. The way you communicate with others affects their opinion of you and their attitude toward you.

Robert Kneschke/Shutterstock.com

*Anutr Yossundara/
Shutterstock.com*

Apply

Case: The Medium and the Message

You work for a medical supply company and are confident in your communication skills. You enjoy meeting with clients face-to-face and listening to their feedback. You are often called on to provide hands-on training to medical office staff. Lately, however, staff cutbacks have required you to do more work over the telephone, through e-mail, or in virtual in-person meetings. Your sales are off, even though you are dealing with the same people.

Case Discussion

1. What might be the cause of this problem?

_____
_____
_____
_____
_____
_____
_____
_____
_____
_____
_____
_____

2. What can you do to solve the problem?

_____
_____
_____
_____
_____
_____
_____
_____
_____
_____
_____
_____
_____

Review

True or False

Indicate *T* if the statement is true or *F* if the statement is false.

1. _____ Attitude has no effect on how a person communicates.
2. _____ Verbal communication refers to spoken words only.
3. _____ Word choice affects how clear your message is.
4. _____ Nonverbal communication cannot take place over the telephone.
5. _____ Attitudes toward others can be conveyed by tone of voice.
6. _____ Nonverbal communication is less important than verbal communication.
7. _____ Listening is part of communication.
8. _____ Listeners can convey their attitude toward a speaker by their body language.
9. _____ Nonverbal communication skills are not relevant to career success.
10. _____ Sometimes a nonverbal message is stronger than a verbal message.

Check Your Understanding

1. Give an example of verbal communication.

_____
_____
_____
_____
_____
_____
_____
_____

2. Give an example of nonverbal communication.

_____
_____
_____
_____
_____
_____
_____
_____

3. Give an example of how attitude affects communication.

_____

_____

_____

_____

_____

_____

_____

4. Explain why listening is an important part of communication.

_____

_____

_____

_____

_____

_____

_____

Journal Writing

What role does communication play in your life? With whom do you communicate most? Is there someone with whom you want or need to communicate more? Which communication skills would you like to improve?

_____

_____

_____

_____

_____

_____

_____

_____

_____

_____

_____

_____

_____

_____

How Well Do You Communicate?

The following quiz can give you some insight into your communication skills. For each pair of statements, place an X by the one that more closely describes you. Respond honestly.

A	Statement A	B	Statement B
	I feel comfortable asking a coworker or fellow student for help with a work problem or school assignment.		I have a hard time asking others for help.
	I feel confident approaching a person in authority for help or to present an idea.		Speaking to people in authority is hard for me. I don't feel comfortable talking about my ideas or asking for help.
	I explain things well. People understand what I am saying.		People often misunderstand me when I am trying to make a point.
	I look directly at others when I am explaining something.		I usually look elsewhere in order to think more easily about what I want to say.
	In a group or at a meeting, I feel comfortable expressing my opinions and sharing ideas.		I don't share my opinions in front of a group, and I dread being asked how I feel about an issue.
	People feel comfortable talking to me.		People rarely start conversations with me.
	I listen carefully when someone is asking me a question.		I often find myself thinking about how I will answer a question, rather than listening carefully.
	I think about how I am coming across when I talk on the phone or via video.		I rarely give thought to how I am communicating on the phone or via video.
	I feel comfortable expressing myself in writing.		I would prefer to talk to someone, rather than write a letter or an e-mail.
	I use my tone of voice to communicate interest in what another person is saying.		I tend to speak in a monotone.
	Total As		**Total Bs**

13 Traits of Valuable Employees

Objectives

- Understand how to learn through observation.
- Recognize traits that form integrity and good character.
- Understand the importance of initiative and good judgment in career success.

Key Terms

observational learning
integrity
good character
dependability
loyalty
trustworthy

honesty
conscientiousness
initiative
good judgment
pros and cons

Integrity and initiative will put you on the path to success.

fizkes/Shutterstock.com

Case

Learning by Observing

Sabrina is one of the top sales representatives for a security firm that installs systems for local businesses. Because of her good performance, she is assigned to train Katie. Katie is the newest member of the sales team. "I'm looking forward to learning your secrets of success, " she tells Sabrina.

Katie is surprised on her first sales call with Sabrina. She had expected to see an outgoing, aggressive salesperson. She thought Sabrina would be self-assured and maybe even a bit pushy. Sabrina is self-assured, but soft-spoken. She has a relaxed and gentle manner.

Katie was curious about Sabrina's methods. "I thought sales work was going to be about the hard sell. I assumed you would have to be pushy and offer deals to get new customers, but your way is different," Katie said.

"No," Sabrina said. "I don't have a high-powered, pushy way of selling. I love the company's products, and they actually sell themselves. I just have to point out the best quality services and good prices we offer." Sabrina explained that she sees her job as a chance to help others obtain peace of mind. "Our track record is our hard sell," she says with a smile. "There are no successful break-ins at the companies that use our systems."

Sabrina and Katie go on several sales calls. The customers seem happy to see Sabrina. Katie notices that Sabrina knows quite a lot about each type of business and its needs. She is able to suggest just the right product and services. She never fails to follow up with clients regularly to ensure ongoing training for new hires and any other support they need.

One day a problem arises. An installation was delayed by up to a week due to a glitch in scheduling. Unfortunately, it is one of Sabrina's new accounts. The owner, Brian, is upset. "I have a vacation planned for two weeks. Our old system broke down. So how am I supposed to relax with my family when I get on the plane tomorrow?"

Katie is surprised that when he takes out his anger on Sabrina, she doesn't place the blame where it belongs: on the contractor they hired to do the installation. Sabrina apologizes without making excuses. "I promise you this problem will be taken care of, so you can enjoy your family vacation," she says calmly.

Back at the office, she tracks down one of the company's engineers and persuades him to install the client's system himself that day. Brian realizes that he has treated Sabrina unfairly. He is impressed with Sabrina's calm and competent response. He tells Sabrina that he will be sure to recommend the company to others for their outstanding service.

Katie trains with Sabrina for a month. On several days, she notices Sabrina seems quieter than usual. Wanting to make sure she is not the source, she asks Sabrina, "Is something bothering you? I hope I'm not the cause."

"Oh, no. You're doing great work," Sabrina assures her. "I'm worried about where I'm going to live. I've been living with my mother in our family home. She's not well and needs to go into assisted living. I'm worried about her being able to adjust and about finding an affordable apartment close to where she will be."

Katie admires Sabrina's ability to focus so clearly on her job when faced with personal problems. Her clients are never aware that Sabrina has anything on her mind except their needs.

Case Analysis

After you have read the case *Learning by Observing*, answer the following questions.

1. Describe Sabrina's attitude toward her job.

_____

_____

_____

2. Why do Sabrina's clients like her?

_____

_____

_____

3. What did Katie observe about Sabrina?

_____

_____

_____

_____

4. List three things Katie can learn from Sabrina and put into practice.

_____

_____

_____

_____

_____

_____

5. Why is learning by observing often better than book learning?

_____

_____

_____

_____

_____

6. Why was Katie surprised to learn that Sabrina had serious problems in her personal life?

_____

_____

_____

_____

7. How did Sabrina exhibit a constructive attitude?

_____

_____

_____

_____

Analyze

You can learn many things from a talented coworker. The manager chose Sabrina to train Katie, the newest member of the sales team. The manager sees qualities in Sabrina that all employees should have.

Observational Learning

Katie watched Sabrina closely. She listened and observed how Sabrina handled relationships. Watching someone to learn how to do something is called observational learning. It can be especially helpful when you start a new job.

When you learn by observing someone, look for the attitudes and behaviors that make them successful. Then work to model those attitudes and behaviors in your way of working. To learn by observing, follow these steps:

- Carefully watch how the person does the job.
- Ask questions.
- Picture the behavior in your mind.
- Remember what was said.
- Practice using the behavior you have observed.

Katie learned from Sabrina that selling doesn't require being aggressive and pushy. She learned not to blame others for mistakes, but instead to work quickly to solve the problem. She saw that Sabrina's proactive approach gained the customer's trust because she got the job done.

Traits of Valued Employees

Employers try to hire people who have integrity or what is sometimes referred to as good character. Some of the traits that show integrity and good character are dependability, loyalty, trustworthiness, honesty, and conscientiousness.

Dependability is the quality of doing what you say you will do and following through on your promises or commitments. When you are dependable, customers know they can count on you. You will do what it takes to keep your commitments. When things go wrong, you will not offer excuses. Instead, you take action to solve the problem. Coworkers know you will do your share of the work and not let tasks fall to them.

Loyalty is the quality of giving support and having a sense of duty toward someone or something. Loyalty to the organization you work for means that you will protect the reputation of the company and its products. Loyalty to coworkers means that you will be respectful and will not gossip and contribute to the rumor mill.

Personal loyalty to someone must be deserved, and it must be reciprocated to maintain a positive relationship. For example, if you have a problem with your supervisor or a coworker, loyalty requires you to discuss your problem directly with the individual. If there is a miscommunication or misunderstanding, try to resolve the issue in a positive way and move on. If you feel in need of advice from a third party, make sure the person you consult is trustworthy. Being **trustworthy** means being deserving of trust or confidence.

Honesty is the quality of telling the truth and being trustworthy. Your coworkers and supervisor have to know that the information you give them about the progress of a project is accurate. Your customers need to trust that the information you give them is true. When you are trusted with company expense money or property, you must use it only according to company-approved purposes. Honesty also means being on time and putting in the hours of work for which you are paid.

Conscientiousness is the quality of being committed to doing what is right and proper. The conscientious worker performs well, whether supervised or not. Conscientious employees have good relationships because supervisors and coworkers know they will do their jobs properly and will not make excuses for mistakes.

Initiative and Good Judgment

In addition to integrity, a worker needs initiative. **Initiative** is the quality of self-motivation—the ability to get the job done on your own. An employee with initiative asks questions, requests help or training when needed, and takes action to solve problems. Initiative is also shown when you offer ideas to improve processes and procedures. Offering to help others to ensure that deadlines and goals are met is an additional way to show your initiative.

Along with initiative comes the need for **good judgment**, the ability to make good decisions. Thinking through the **pros and cons**, the arguments for and against something, and the potential outcome shows good judgment. Thinking before you speak is another attribute of having good judgment. Knowing how far to go on your own and when to seek permission is a matter of judgment. You wouldn't want to do anything that is not authorized by your company's management. Nor would you want to make decisions without notifying your supervisor or team members. This is where observational learning comes in. Observing how things are done in your workplace, especially by your supervisor and successful coworkers, will help you develop good judgment.

Sabrina's company is lucky to have her as a sales representative. Her personal qualities and constructive attitude are an asset to the business. Try to imagine Sabrina being consistently late for work or failing to show up for an appointment. Can you picture her joining in gossip about another employee or complaining about the company to a customer? Sabrina's human relations skills will take her far.

Party people studio/Shutterstock.com

Apply

Case: Budget Cuts

fizkes/Shutterstock.com

Your department has been informed of a cost-cutting initiative. The department's expenses across the board are over budget. Purchase of office supplies has increased due to usage of printing and photocopy paper.

There is no obvious explanation for these problems, such as an increase in business. In fact, it is the slow season and business has decreased for the past two months. The supervisor calls the staff together to talk about how costs can be brought down.

Case Analysis

1. List three suggestions to bring costs down.

_____
_____
_____
_____
_____
_____

2. How might an "employee of the month" program help bring costs down?

_____
_____
_____
_____
_____
_____

3. List five qualities that the employee must have to make the cost reduction plan work.

_____
_____
_____
_____
_____
_____
_____
_____
_____

Review

True or False

Indicate *T* if the statement is true or *F* if the statement is false.

1. _____ Observational learning is helpful when a person starts a new job.
2. _____ Dependability is only important in relationships with customers.
3. _____ Loyalty is one of the reasons employees should avoid contributing to the rumor mill.
4. _____ Thinking through the pros and cons is a way to make good decisions.
5. _____ Offering ideas for improvements shows an employee's initiative.
6. _____ Being loyal means you should not discuss a problem with your supervisor.
7. _____ Conscientious workers need close supervision.
8. _____ In the work world, being a good person is enough to get ahead.
9. _____ An employee with initiative must also use good judgment.
10. _____ Integrity, initiative, and honesty are traits of a valuable employee.

Check Your Understanding

1. Describe how observational learning works.

_____

_____

_____

_____

_____

_____

_____

2. List four traits that contribute to integrity.

_____

_____

_____

_____

_____

_____

_____

_____

3. Describe initiative.

_____

_____

_____

_____

_____

_____

_____

4. How do dependability, loyalty, trustworthiness, honesty, and conscientiousness contribute to a constructive attitude?

_____

_____

_____

_____

_____

_____

_____

Journal Writing

1. Identify the traits you have that give you a constructive attitude. What additional traits would you like to acquire?

_____
_____
_____
_____
_____
_____
_____
_____
_____
_____
_____
_____
_____
_____
_____
_____
_____
_____

2. List three things you learned through observation. What did this learning help you achieve?

_____
_____
_____
_____
_____
_____
_____
_____
_____
_____
_____
_____
_____
_____
_____
_____
_____
_____
_____

Are You a Valuable Employee?

Evaluate the personal qualities that make you a valuable employee. Rate yourself on each quality in the list. Use the following scale:

5 = always, 4 = usually, 3 = sometimes, 2 = rarely, 1 = never

Dependability

_____ My supervisor/instructors can count on me to do a job/assignment conscientiously.

_____ When I have a scheduled time to be someplace, I arrive on time.

_____ I do my share of every job/group project.

Loyalty

_____ I avoid making negative comments about other people.

_____ Secrets are safe with me.

_____ I refuse to gossip or spread rumors.

_____ I remain true to my ideals.

Honesty

_____ If I am paid to do a job, I make sure I put in the time expected.

_____ I do not use the property of others without permission.

_____ People can count on me to be truthful.

Conscientiousness

_____ I do my work without needing to be closely supervised.

_____ I take pride in my work.

_____ I know what is expected of me.

Initiative

_____ I try to do just a little bit more than is expected.

_____ I am eager to learn new things.

_____ I make suggestions that will help others even if I don't directly benefit.

Make a list of the items on which you gave yourself a 1 or 2 rating and the related personal quality. Next to each, give a reason your rating is low and how you can improve.

14 Strategies for a Positive Work Attitude

Objectives

- Define the three components of work attitude.
- List ten strategies for maintaining a positive work attitude.

Key Terms

work attitude
self-esteem
self-confidence
work ethic
prioritizing
opportunity

Develop strategies to help you maintain a positive attitude at work.

Sasirin pamas/Shutterstock.com

Case

The Right Job

Mardryka is a nurse's aide at a local nursing home. She works the evening shift, from 3 p.m. to 11 p.m. She usually arrives 15 minutes early for her shift. Those extra minutes give her time to talk to the aide from the previous shift. She can find out whether any of the patients on her floor are having difficulty. Sometimes, patient problems during the day mean that some of the duties of the day shift have to be handled in the evening. Today is one of those days. Mardryka receives a quick briefing and plans how she will organize her time to fit in everything that needs to be done.

As Mardryka enters the hall, Eileen calls to her. Mardryka waves hello, but keeps on walking. Eileen, the senior aide on the evening shift, always has a complaint. As Mardryka walks down the hall, Eileen catches up with her.

"It's just you and me again tonight," Eileen says. "That darn Zachary called. One of his kids has the flu, and he can't take her to the sitter's. I'm getting sick and tired of this! I'll bet it's just an excuse to stay home and watch TV. I'll tell you…"

Mardryka cuts her short, trying to keep the irritation out of her voice. "Zachary hardly ever takes time off, Eileen. Why would you doubt his excuse? It's hard raising three young kids alone, and I admire him for working so hard to support them. Besides, the flu can be dangerous to an elderly person. Zachary should stay home rather than take the chance of spreading infection."

"Just makes more work for us," Eileen grumbles.

Mardryka starts the evening routine. Her patients are glad to see her. She always greets them pleasantly. When she has the time, she spends a few extra minutes chatting with them. Mardryka knows that many of these people rarely have visitors. Conversation and attention are important to them.

Some patients are ill and in pain. Some have problems with memory. At times, a patient yells at an aide. Mardryka sometimes hears Eileen yell back. Mardryka realizes that the patients' anger is not directed at her personally. She knows they are angry at their illness and their inability to cope. Mardryka tries to put herself in their place. She treats all her patients as she would want to be treated.

Latoya is the registered nurse in charge on the evening shift. Latoya spends part of every evening checking Eileen's work, even though Eileen is the senior aide. Latoya plans to talk to Eileen about considering a career change. She is worried that Eileen isn't happy in the job and it is affecting her attitude. An aide cannot be irritable or make mistakes in a nursing home.

Latoya considers Mardryka "her right arm." She often tells her, "I don't know what I would do without you." Mardryka has volunteered to attend in-service training sessions on her own time. She has asked to borrow Latoya's nursing journals. Latoya is encouraging Mardryka to attend nursing school.

Case Analysis

After you have read the case *The Right Job,* answer the following questions.

1. Describe Mardryka's attitude toward her job.

_____

_____

_____

2. Describe Eileen's attitude toward her job.

_____

_____

_____

_____

3. What does Mardryka do to make Latoya depend on her and encourage her career in nursing?

_____

_____

_____

_____

4. How does high self-esteem help Mardryka have a positive attitude at work?

_____

_____

_____

_____

_____

5. What advice would you give to Eileen to help her improve her attitude toward the work she is doing?

_____

_____

_____

_____

6. Give an example to illustrate each of the strategies for improving Eileen's attitude.

_____

_____

_____

_____

_____

_____

Analyze

Everyone's life—home, school, work, and social—is full of ups and downs. It is normal to feel positive at times and negative at other times. How can you stay positive at work? First, understand yourself and what forms your attitudes. Then develop strategies to help you maintain a positive attitude at work.

Work Attitudes

Your **work attitude** has three components: attitude toward self, attitude toward work, and attitude toward the workplace.

Attitude Toward Self

Your level of self-esteem has a major effect on how you feel about work. **Self-esteem** is the measure of how you feel about yourself. You have strong feelings of self-worth and self-confidence when your self-esteem is high. When you have **self-confidence**, you feel sure of your abilities. You know you can handle any challenge that comes your way.

When your self-esteem and confidence are high, you see others as peers and coworkers. You do not feel threatened by others who have more skills, experience, or knowledge than you. Instead, you develop good relationships so you can learn from them.

When your self-esteem is high, it is easier to sympathize with others and understand what they are feeling. People with low self-esteem tend to focus on themselves and their own feelings. When your self-esteem is low, you tend to see more accomplished people as threats. Your lack of self-confidence makes you feel you cannot rise to their level of success or competence.

Think about Eileen's and Mardryka's responses to Zachary's absence. Eileen attacks Zachary and focuses on herself—she now has more work to do. Mardryka's self-esteem enables her to defend Zachary. She doesn't need to put down another person to feel good about herself because she already feels good about herself. She believes Zachary's reason for being absent and gives him credit for thinking about the welfare of the patients. Instead of being angry about doing more work, she feels good about filling in for Zachary.

Attitude Toward Work

A person's attitude toward their work affects their **work ethic**, which can be strong or weak. People with a strong work ethic believe that the act of working is important. They attach a moral value to hard work and do their best no matter what job they are doing. They feel that the work itself is rewarding. People with a strong work ethic are willing to pitch in when problems arise and are willing to put in extra hours. People with a weak work ethic have the opposite traits.

When Eileen heard that Zachary was not coming in, she was angry. She did not want to do any extra work. Eileen dislikes her work. Her work ethic is poor.

Attitude Toward Your Workplace

How you feel about the company or organization you work for is a key factor in how you feel about your job. If you respect the organization, the people, and the company's products or services, you are proud of what you do. This pride contributes to self-esteem and self-confidence.

If, like Eileen, you don't feel good about your work and your workplace, you need to give thought to the reasons. Mardryka had a positive attitude toward the nursing home. She was committed to the nursing home's professional goal of serving elderly people. Doing the job means more to Mardryka than just earning a paycheck. On the other hand, Eileen's negative attitude led Latoya to question whether she was in the right job.

No job is perfect, and every job has its ups and downs. It is never easy to be positive all the time. The following are ten strategies that many people use to maintain a positive attitude.

1. Examine Your Attitude Regularly

Think about your day at work. Think about your relationships with your coworkers and supervisors. Is your attitude positive or negative? constructive or destructive?

If your attitude is negative, try to determine why. Ask yourself these questions:

- Am I unsuited for my job?
- Are personal problems interfering with my work performance?
- Do I dislike my coworkers or supervisor?
- Do I need more training to perform my tasks effectively?
- How can I change destructive attitudes to constructive ones?

If your attitude is positive, are you projecting that attitude to others? Most likely, you will discover one or two areas where you need to adjust your attitude. Ask yourself these questions:

- How would my supervisor describe me?
- How would my coworkers rate my human relations skills?

You may love your job but find that certain people or tasks cause you problems. When you find a problem, you can work to fix it.

2. Balance Work with Personal Life

All work and no play is not healthy, but all play and no work is not good either. Only you can decide how to allocate your time and energy. Figure out a balance that works for you. This is called prioritizing, which means managing the order of importance of various aspects of your work and personal life. For example, is it more important to spend time with your friends during the week or to feel rested and alert at work the next day? If spending weekends with friends is enough socializing for you, then you are making work a priority. When you know your priorities, it is easier to make the decisions that are right for you.

When you are at home, focus on your family and friends. Leave work problems at work. Similarly, when at work, put home problems on a back burner. Focus on your work. If you do not feel stressed about your priorities, it is easier to maintain a positive attitude toward work.

3. Focus on the Positive

If one aspect of your job gets you down, don't let it overshadow the positive aspects. Mardryka probably did not enjoy working with cranky patients, but her focus was on the good she could do each day. She used her skills to make them feel better. It gave her satisfaction to help others, and she felt good about her job.

Focus on the positive in your work and in your relationships on the job. Remember, you can have good working relationships with everyone, even with those who differ from you in many ways. Focus on the values and goals you share, such as building a productive department.

When you have differences with others or have to solve problems you did not cause, rely on your constructive attitude and work ethic to make the best of the situation. You will get satisfaction out of helping your peers and your employer.

4. Communicate

Practice good listening and communication skills every day. Be sure you say what you mean and that you hear what others are saying. When you feel misunderstood or have trouble understanding, it is hard to keep a positive attitude.

Ask questions when you do not understand something. If you are giving directions, make sure your listeners understand you. Ask them to repeat your instructions back to you or to explain what you just told them.

5. Turn Unexpected Changes into Opportunities

Human beings are creatures of habit. We are comfortable with the familiar—friends, supervisors, coworkers, routines, foods. Change, however, is an inevitable part of life. If you stay in a job long enough, some changes are sure to happen. Companies are bought and sold. Managers and coworkers come and go. Your duties change. New company policies go into effect.

Your first reaction to changes at work may be negative. However, it is essential to adapt to change and remain positive. You might not like a new boss or a new assignment. Be honest if something is bothering you, and talk to your supervisor about it. Focus on what you can learn. Every new situation can be a learning experience if you are open to new challenges. Adopt the attitude that every change presents an opportunity, a new set of circumstances that makes it possible for you to do or learn something. Even when the change does not appear to be beneficial to you, try to use it as an opportunity to grow as an individual.

6. Educate Yourself

It is tough to be positive if you are having trouble doing your job. Education is the key to being confident about your abilities. You can read the writings of experts in the field and use the vast online resources that are available.

Continuing education, training, courses, and certifications outside of a formal education setting are necessary for advancement in many careers. You can enroll in courses and certification programs outside of the formal education system to acquire additional skills and credentials. Whether or not it is required, education is never wasted. Be a lifelong learner. The more you learn, the more confident you will be.

7. Maintain Your Interest

In the first months on a job, you are learning new things. The excitement and challenge keep you interested, and your attitude is positive.

As time goes on, you might begin to feel bored. You might feel that you are not being challenged, or that the work is not as satisfying as you expected. If this happens, look for ways to regain the interest you once felt. Analyze your job duties. Look for areas where you can take more initiative. Come up with new ideas for doing routine tasks.

Supervisors count on workers with initiative and enthusiasm to show new employees the ropes. If Latoya were looking for an employee to train a newly hired aide, would she ask Mardryka or Eileen? Eileen may be the senior aide, but she no longer has any enthusiasm for her job. Her negative attitude affects her relationships with the patients, supervisors, and other aides. Mardryka would be the obvious choice, and both she and the new employee would benefit from the experience.

8. Have a Sense of Humor

Humor can help your outlook on almost anything. Taking yourself and others too seriously will not solve problems. It may cause you to dwell on mistakes or focus on the negative side of situations that cannot be changed.

Maintaining a sense of humor at work means having the ability to see the lighter side of situations. People with a good sense of humor can say just the right thing to break the tension. Your sense of humor can help you keep a balanced outlook when confronted with problems, conflicts, or unexpected changes at work.

9. Take Care of Your Health

Good health habits can affect your job performance and your attitude. A healthy diet and exercise combined with good sleeping habits help you cope with everyday stress. The better you feel, the easier it is to stay positive.

The negative effects of poor health habits might not happen immediately; but over time, such habits can reduce your productivity on the job. Staying up late every night will affect your ability to be alert the next day. A lack of exercise may result in a buildup of tensions and lack of energy. Any type of substance abuse will impair your ability to perform.

If you do not already practice a health regimen, put yourself on a path to change bad habits and adopt a health-conscious lifestyle.

10. Dress for Success

Your attitude and your appearance are related. If you look good, you are more likely to feel good about yourself. Everyone has a favorite outfit that can improve a mood instantly. Choose clothes that are appropriate for your position and the kind of work you do.

Never forget that your appearance affects others' opinions of you and their reactions to you. People have a lifetime of experiences, exposure to cultural norms, and personal opinions that influence their reactions to others. A supervisor might make decisions about your future based on how you dress and your grooming. This may be based on reality or completely off the mark, and you may or may not ever know about it.

The supervisor may not even be aware of how much influence these ingrained opinions are having in their own actions. Being aware of the dress code for your job, whether formal or informal, is part of adjusting to expectations. If you work in an organization where a certain level of conformity of dress is the norm, it might be a good decision to fall in line. It is up to you to show your feelings about yourself, your position, and your workplace by presenting an appropriate image.

Pressmaster/Shutterstock.com

Andy Dean Photography/ Shutterstock.com

Apply

Case: Torn Between Priorities

You are in competition for a promotion at work. At the same time, your family is moving to a new home. Your boss keeps asking you to come in on Saturdays to help with a special project. Your family is counting on you to organize the move and help pack. You are exhausted because of the physical and mental demands that are being placed on you. You are torn between your need to spend time at home and your desire to advance.

Case Discussion

1. List three options for dealing with your job situation.

_____
_____
_____
_____
_____
_____
_____
_____
_____

2. List the option you would choose, and explain why you would choose it.

_____
_____
_____
_____
_____
_____
_____
_____
_____
_____
_____
_____
_____
_____
_____
_____

Review

True or False

Indicate *T* if the statement is true or *F* if the statement is false.

1. _____ A person in the proper job will always be positive about that job.
2. _____ Low self-esteem can interfere with job performance.
3. _____ There is one right way to balance the demands of work and home.
4. _____ Supervisors always let employees know about any negative opinions that may affect decisions about the employees' future.
5. _____ Most people respond happily to unexpected changes in their life.
6. _____ The only way to learn something new is to return to school.
7. _____ A worker's initiative and interest may lessen after some time on the job.
8. _____ Having a sense of humor at work means making fun of coworkers.
9. _____ A poor diet and lack of exercise will sap your energy and make it harder to be productive.
10. _____ People often judge others by their appearance.

Check Your Understanding

1. List the three components of work attitude.

_____

_____

_____

_____

_____

_____

_____

_____

_____

_____

2. Why is it a good idea to examine your attitude regularly?

_____

_____

_____

_____

_____

_____

_____

_____

3. List the ten strategies you can use to improve your attitude.

_____

_____

_____

_____

_____

_____

_____

_____

_____

_____

_____

_____

_____

Journal Writing

Name_____

1. Your work attitude includes attitude toward self, work, and the workplace. Analyze your work attitude. If you do not work, analyze your attitude toward school instead.

_____

_____

_____

_____

_____

_____

_____

_____

_____

_____

_____

2. Describe a challenging situation when you needed to maintain a positive attitude, even though it was difficult. What strategies did you use?

_____

_____

_____

_____

_____

_____

_____

_____

_____

_____

_____

3. Describe how you could use each of the ten strategies to improve your attitude.

_____

_____

_____

_____

_____

_____

_____

_____

_____

_____

15 Succeeding in a New Job

Objectives

- Describe techniques for making a smooth adjustment to a new job.
- Define what is meant by a probation period for new workers.
- Understand areas of adjustment on a new job and how to handle them.
- Explain written and unwritten rules in organizations.

Key Terms

probation period
orientation
on-the-job training
status quo
performance review
goal setting

performance objectives
company policies
company procedures
unwritten rules
organizational culture

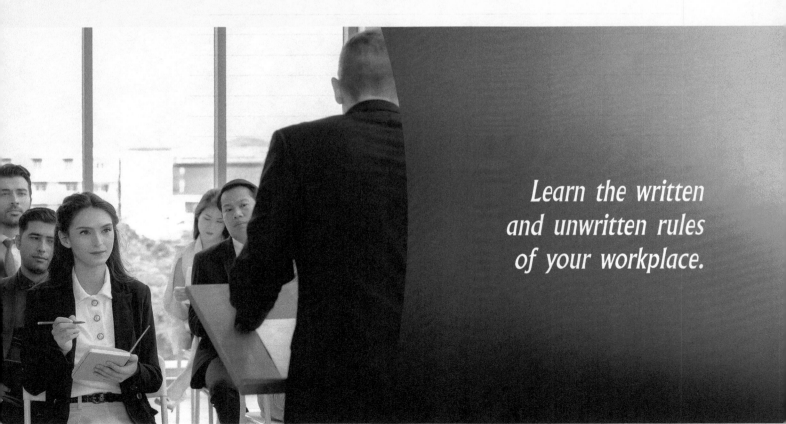

Learn the written and unwritten rules of your workplace.

Parinya Maneenate/Shutterstock.com

Case

The Newest Worker

Erica is starting a career in food service in a large city hospital. Her supervisor, Donna, greets her and says, "Welcome, we're happy to have you on board. You will start with three days of training to learn the basics of hospital food service. Then you will follow one of our staff on rounds to serve the patients' lunch and dinner."

After three days, Erica feels she understands the basics of how the right food from the kitchen gets to each patient according to their dietary needs. Now Erica is assigned to follow Manny on lunchtime rounds. Manny is polite and careful in explaining the job to Erica, but is not very friendly. Erica learns that making sure patients get the right trays, correcting mistakes made by the kitchen, and trying to please everyone is more challenging than she would have thought. At their lunch break, Manny seems distant and goes off to sit with a group in the cafeteria.

Erica likes the work, but she is getting lonely. After a week, Erica's training moves to food preparation. Like Manny, her coworkers are polite, but they don't seem very interested in her. She misses conversation and laughing and joking with colleagues while they work, as she did when she worked in retail. "It is a hospital, after all. People need to be cheerful," Erica thinks to herself.

After three months, Erica has gone through every step of food service at the hospital, but she hasn't made one good friend. On her three-month anniversary, Donna calls Erica into her office and says, "Congratulations! You have passed the probation period. You are now officially a member of the food service department."

At the next staff meeting, Donna announces Erica's new status as Food Service Associate. The group applauds enthusiastically. That day, Manny and some others ask Erica to join them at lunch. Erica gladly accepts.

As they stand in the lunch line, Erica asks, "Why have you guys been so unfriendly?"

Manny asks, "What do you mean?"

"Well," says Erica, "you wouldn't chat with me while we were delivering trays; and before today, you ignored me at lunchtime."

Manny replies, "I'm sorry if we seemed unfriendly. We don't have time to chat while we are preparing food and serving patients. It is so important to get the right food to the right patient. If not, they might have a bad reaction. They also deserve quick service and hot food, and we need to notice if they're not eating. So, we all try to focus only on our work while serving patients."

"And what about lunchtime?" asks Erica.

Manny says, "To be honest, a lot of new people don't make it through the probation period. We never know who will mess up and be let go or who will decide they don't like working in a hospital after all. You'd be surprised. Some people are gone after a short time. So, I guess we wait to see who stays around before we start making friends. I'm sorry you got the wrong impression. We really like you."

Erica feels much better now. She realizes that adjusting to her new job had many unexpected challenges.

Case Analysis

After you have read the case *The Newest Worker,* answer the following questions.

1. What is your reaction to this case?

_____

_____

2. Do you think Donna was a good manager?

_____

_____

3. If you were in Erica's situation, what would you do?

_____

_____

4. Do you think a probation period is a good idea? Why or why not?

_____

_____

_____

5. Why would a company want to give you training even if you have already been trained?

_____

_____

_____

6. Why might coworkers keep a distance from a new person?

_____

_____

7. Would you want to work for a company that has a probation period? Why or why not?

_____

_____

_____

_____

_____

Analyze

Starting a new job can be a stressful time. It is exciting to meet new people and learn new skills. On the other hand, it is human nature to be uncomfortable in new situations and to worry about failing.

Good human relations skills can ease your entry into a new job. A positive attitude will help as you establish relationships with new coworkers. Learning the written and unwritten rules of your workplace will help you adjust and fit in with your new work environment.

Probation Period

Many workplaces have a probation period for new employees. This is a period of time during which an employee is hired, but performance is evaluated to determine if employment will be permanent. It allows the hiring manager to assess the employee's ability to do the job satisfactorily. Probation usually lasts between 30 and 90 days. The understanding between the employer and employee is that the employee may be let go at the end of the probation period without further notice. It may also include delayed eligibility for benefits such as health insurance and vacation leave.

Probation protects the employer in the event that their initial evaluation of a job candidate proves incorrect. They need to be able to see whether the person can perform the job. If the person does not work out, the company needs an easy way to let the person go. As a job candidate, you should always be informed of this policy before accepting a position. Once you pass probation, you are officially a member of the team and are eligible for all benefits and opportunities for growth.

Orientation and Training

Orientation for new employees is usually a program to provide information about the organization, its mission, and its policies. It also describes information about employee benefits, such as health insurance and paid time off.

New employees may also receive training for a period of time. This may be formal or informal time spent with coworkers or professional training instructors. This on-the-job training is designed to familiarize new employees with the specific skills, processes, and procedures required for the job. Even if you are experienced in your area, you may need training specific to the organization's way of doing things. Training might also include using technology systems specific to the job.

Keep in mind that, even with training, you might not be told the rules, procedures, and guidelines all at once. You might be caught by surprise when told that you have done or said the wrong thing. This is part of the learning experience and should be taken in stride. If the job is a good fit for you, the stress of the adjustment period will diminish as long as you maintain a positive attitude.

Coworkers and the New Worker

Anything that changes the status quo, the current state of affairs and how things are routinely done, will be questioned by the current staff. Even if a department desperately needs more workers, the existing workers have many questions. Is the new worker nice? Will the person do a good job? Will the new person make mistakes and ruin the reputation of the company? Will the new worker be better than me and get my job or the promotion I want?

Some workplaces are very warm and friendly. Others are tense and fast-paced. If a person on staff applied for the position for which you were hired, your new coworkers may treat you with suspicion. Be patient if they are distant for a while. Don't jump to negative conclusions. Erica did the right thing by waiting to see how her coworkers treated her once she was officially a part of the team.

Remember that you do not have to be friends with your coworkers, but you do need to have good working relationships. All coworkers should treat you with respect. Use your communication and human relations skills to get to know your coworkers and supervisor, and be patient. Relationships are formed over time.

Feedback and Review

As a student, you are accustomed to receiving frequent feedback on your work in the form of grades. In the workplace, how often you receive feedback and how it is given depends on the supervisor's or manager's work style. When you start a job, take the initiative to ask for feedback if you don't get it. In many workplaces, formal reviews are required once or twice a year. This is known as a performance review, a formal evaluation of an employee's work and productivity.

Most companies that require formal reviews have a goal-setting process. Goal setting is a procedure that requires the supervisor and each worker to agree on the employee's performance objectives. The performance objectives define what is expected of the employee on specific projects or work tasks within a set period of time. When employees are clear on how they will be evaluated, they feel reassured that the process will be fair.

Typically, the supervisor has a private meeting with each worker at least twice a year. At this meeting, the supervisor and worker discuss the review. The employee is usually encouraged to take an active role. If you receive criticism on your performance or when you make a mistake, use your communication skills to ask for help and make sure you understand.

One of the best things you can do is learn how to take criticism in stride. Have a positive attitude toward constructive comments from supervisors or coworkers. You should thank the person for the helpful comments and vow to do better. When you feel that you have been unfairly evaluated or criticized, take the initiative to have a meeting to express your view and gain an understanding of the supervisor's point of view. Always approach these situations with a constructive attitude. When necessary, seek the advice or support of others to ensure you are treated fairly.

Keep in mind that not all organizations have a process for formal goal setting and performance review. Some managers make expectations very clear and are comfortable with providing constructive feedback. Others are more likely to be critical than to offer praise. Observing how your manager handles the job of training and guiding you and your coworkers will help you adapt.

Learn the Rules

Workplaces have many rules, both written and unwritten. **Company policies** are written rules of conduct within an organization outlining the responsibilities of both employees and the employer. **Company procedures** are work guidelines and processes that may be written or unwritten. Procedures cover everything from how to do specific work tasks to rules of conduct, such as what to do if you wake up ill and can't make it to work.

Most workplaces also have **unwritten rules**. These are guidelines for behavior that every employee seems to know, although they are not part of the written company policies. These rules are part of the **organizational culture**—the values, behavioral expectations, and practices that guide and inform the actions of employees. You learn these rules through interaction with your coworkers and managers. As a result, you feel more comfortable and able to fit in with your coworkers and the organization as a whole. Do people stand in the hallway and chat, or do they only socialize during lunch and breaks? Is it okay to be a little noisy, or does everyone speak in hushed tones? Do people socialize together after work or only during work hours? If you are unsure about the unwritten rules, ask your supervisor or a friendly coworker.

Rawpixel/Shutterstock.com

Arts Illustrated Studios/
Shutterstock.com

Apply

Case: A Difficult Adjustment

You have been at your new job for six months and are starting to feel comfortable with the work and with your coworkers. You began with high hopes and a positive attitude. You expected an initial adjustment period, but were not prepared for the lack of friendliness from your coworkers. You notice that they go out to lunch to celebrate each other's birthdays. You have overheard conversations about getting together after work, but have not been invited to these occasions either. You are beginning to wonder: is it me or is it them? You're not sure that you want to be a part of their group, even if they decide to let you in. You find yourself getting irritable and snapping at coworkers when they talk to you. You are beginning to dread going to work even though you like your job.

Case Analysis

1. List three options for dealing with your job situation.

_____
_____
_____
_____
_____
_____
_____
_____
_____

2. List the option you would choose, and explain why you would choose it.

_____
_____
_____
_____
_____
_____
_____
_____
_____
_____
_____

Review

True or False

Indicate *T* if the statement is true or *F* if the statement is false.

1. _____ Starting a new job is stressful for most people.

2. _____ Probation is a good time to take time off because a worker isn't really on staff yet.

3. _____ During orientation, a new worker learns about the company and its rules.

4. _____ Company procedures may be written or unwritten.

5. _____ Adding a new worker can upset the existing workers, even if they desperately need the added help.

6. _____ Setting performance objectives is useful in having a fair performance review.

7. _____ Feedback is always regularly given to employees by their supervisors and managers.

8. _____ The status quo refers to the routine way of doing things.

9. _____ The unwritten rules of the workplace can be learned from observing the behavior of others.

10. _____ People can do a good job at work, even if they are not friends with their coworkers.

Check Your Understanding

1. Describe probation in the workplace.

_____

_____

_____

_____

_____

2. Why is it important to observe organizational culture?

_____

_____

_____

_____

_____

3. How would you act if you were new on a job and your coworkers were distant?

_____

_____

_____

_____

_____

_____

4. Why is it important for the employee and supervisor to agree on performance objectives?

_____

_____

_____

_____

_____

5. How can you learn the unwritten rules of the workplace?

_____

_____

_____

_____

_____

Journal Writing

Think of a time when you were a new person in a job, school, committee, or some other group. What feelings did you experience? Were people friendly or distant? How did you react? What did you do to get to know people? What did people do to welcome you?

_____
_____
_____
_____
_____
_____
_____
_____
_____
_____
_____
_____
_____
_____
_____
_____
_____
_____
_____
_____
_____
_____
_____
_____
_____
_____
_____
_____
_____
_____
_____
_____
_____

16 Being a Reliable Employee

Objectives

- Understand the importance of being on time.
- Explain the negative impact of absenteeism and tardiness.
- Understand how companies handle time and attendance.
- List ways to make sure you are on time.

Key Terms

reliable
absenteeism
tardiness
unprofessional
disciplinary action
flextime
organizational culture
paid leave

Absenteeism and tardiness negatively affect your career.

LarsZ/Shutterstock.com

Case

Time and Attendance

Blake rushes through the front door of the home gym equipment and fitness center where he works. In his haste, he almost crashes into a customer on her way out. His manager, Richard, stands inside the door, arms crossed, looking very displeased.

"I'm really sorry, Rich." Blake tries to catch his breath. "It's just that my alarm didn't go off and…"

"Save the explanation. I'm not interested," Richard replies. "Did you recognize that customer you almost knocked over as you raced in?"

"I guess I didn't really notice. Oh, no!" Blake smacks his head. "I forgot! I was going to show Deborah Hunter the new rowing machine we just got in stock."

"Well, she was here right on time," says Richard. "When I explained that you weren't here and the equipment was still crated downstairs, she left. Didn't I ask you to set that up yesterday? What happened?"

"I was tied up with training sessions most of the day. And then, well, I guess I left a little early."

"How early is a little early?" Richard asked. "Ten minutes? Two hours?"

"It's just that I had these tickets to the game, and with the traffic and all. I didn't leave *too* early." Even as he says it, Blake knows he is in big trouble this time.

"Blake, you know this equipment better than any other person. I rely on you. When you're here, you are the best; but that's the problem. You are almost never here! I was looking over your attendance record. You are late almost half the time, and I can count on you missing work entirely at least once every two weeks. Do you realize that in the past three months, you've called in sick on six Mondays and twice on Friday?

"I think my policies on absenteeism and tardiness are pretty liberal," Richard continued. "I know my employees have lives outside of work, and I try to be lenient. However, you have abused my patience.

"Blake, I really hate to do this; but if you do not have 100% attendance and timely arrival for the next month, I will have to let you go."

Case Analysis

After you have read the case *Time and Attendance,* answer the following questions.

1. What is your reaction to this case?

_____

_____

2. What is Blake's attitude toward his job?

_____

_____

3. What effect does Blake's behavior have on his job performance?

_____

_____

_____

4. Is Richard justified in criticizing Blake?

_____

_____

_____

5. Name two things that did not get done because of Blake's tardiness.

_____

_____

_____

6. What do you think of Blake's story concerning tickets to the game?

_____

_____

_____

7. What effect might Blake's absenteeism and tardiness have on his coworkers?

_____

_____

_____

8. What effect could Blake's absenteeism and tardiness have on the success of the business?

_____

_____

_____

9. What advice would you give Blake?

_____

_____

_____

Analyze

One of the most important characteristics valued by employers is reliability. Being reliable means you can be trusted and depended on to keep your obligations. Two of the main measures of reliability in the workplace are absenteeism and tardiness. Absenteeism is being absent from work. Tardiness is arriving late to work. No matter how good you are at your job, if you cannot be relied on to be there, and be on time, you will sabotage your path to success.

An employee who is chronically late or takes too many days off may be judged as unprofessional. This means they are acting in ways that do not meet the high standards of an excellent worker. Such employees may be subject to disciplinary action. Disciplinary action is a formal response to misbehavior or rule breaking at work. It may take the form of a verbal warning, a written warning, a suspension, or termination.

Follow Time Rules and Policies

Reliable employees know their assigned work hours and follow them unless they have approval for time off or late arrival. Individual arrangements may be made upon request to a supervisor or Human Resources to accommodate an employee's special circumstances. Many companies also offer flextime, a policy that allows workers to vary their arrival and departure within a specified time period at the start and end of the workday.

Employees are also given guidelines and rules about whom to notify and how to notify the company on days when they are going to be late for work or take a day off. Planned time off may include doctor appointments, vacation leave, personal leave, and sick leave. Unplanned time off or tardiness may involve unexpected illness of the employee or a family member, other family obligations, transportation problems, and any number of other reasons.

When you have to miss work or arrive late, always consider the impact of your actions on others and the impression you are making on management. In addition to the need to get the work done, employers are conscious of the need to be fair to all employees. Allowing one person to be absent or arrive late frequently may lead others to wonder why they are rushing to be on time. For this reason, it is unwise to assume that an employer will or should accept "good reasons" for your absence or tardiness if it becomes chronic. They will expect you to take responsibility for handling the situation that is causing the problem. It is up to you to avoid jeopardizing your job, no matter what the cause.

Understand the Cultural Environment

You learned earlier about the organizational culture, the values, behavioral expectations, and practices that guide and inform the actions of employees. Organizations and managers vary in the degree of structure placed on arrival and leave time. Some pay close attention to time spent away from the employee's workstation. Others are more lenient. Picking up on these cues is critically important when you settle into a new job.

Consider your employer's definition of "start time." If you are just stepping into the building at your 9 a.m. start time or stopping in the employee lounge for breakfast, it might be okay if this is the norm at your place of work. If you work in a more structured environment where work starts promptly at the appointed time, take this into consideration. Do not make assumptions or bring habits from one workplace to another—especially if you leave a place that had loose structure for one that is more disciplined.

It is always best to set high standards for yourself when it comes to being present and being on time. It is always up to you to adjust to expectations. Thinking the workplace should adjust to your habits or needs is a big mistake.

Be Organized and Productive

Many successful people adopt the habit of being early. Scheduling an extra 15 or 20 minutes at the start of your schedule is a good way to avoid the stress of running late. It also gives you the opportunity to settle in or chat with a colleague without impacting your productivity.

Highly productive employees organize themselves before they leave work for the day. This is important, especially if your job is hectic. Stopping at the end of the day to make a list, plan the next day's work, and organize your workstation enables you to start fresh and relaxed. Managers notice these kinds of habits, whether or not they ever mention it.

If you have a job in which you serve customers, you will need to be ready to begin working immediately at the start of business. Lateness will result in poor customer service. Either no one will be there to serve customers, or your coworkers will have to cover for you. The result may be angry customers who decide to never return to your business.

Remember what you learned about feedback from supervisors and managers. Some bring issues to your attention early and let you correct your behavior. Others may let it go until they find it intolerable, as happened with Richard and Blake. By the time Richard spoke to Blake, he was ready to fire him.

Official Policies for Time Off

Most large organizations have official policies for time off. Sometimes very small companies do not have written policies. In that case, ask what the policies are and write them down for future reference.

Most businesses have specific policies on how long breaks and lunchtimes are and when they can be taken. In some jobs, workers have a required amount of time for lunch and breaks during the day. The amount of time and when you are to take it will be specified by your employer. If you are not clear about the policy, be sure to ask. Returning from lunch and breaks on time is as important as arriving at work on time.

Paid Leave

Organizations realize that their workers need to take time off. Paid leave is time off with pay, which may include vacation, sick leave, and time off for certain holidays or personal business. It is always wise to give advance notice of planned use of your paid leave. Policies may require you to submit an official request or get your manager's approval for the days you want to take off when known in advance.

Emergency Absences

Employers realize that sickness, accidents, and other types of emergencies occur. Weather can delay flights returning from vacation, and automobile accidents can keep you from getting to work. The most important first step is to call your supervisor as soon as you know you have a problem getting to work.

Make sure you know the policy for handling these situations. If you are too ill to go to work, know who to contact, what method to use, and communicate as early as possible. If you can help make arrangements for getting something done or having someone fill in for you, take the extra step to do so. This is an opportunity to show your constructive attitude.

Avoid Tardiness

There are several strategies you can use to avoid tardiness.
- **Commit yourself to being at work on time every day, after every break, and after lunch.** No excuses.
- **Allow enough time to get ready for work.** Do not try to do too many things in the morning. Focus on getting ready and getting out of the house.
- **Use 15 minutes before your actual start time as your goal arrival time.** This extra time allows you to hang up your coat, visit the restroom, get to your desk, and organize your work for the day.
- **Leave extra time for the commute to work.** If you know it takes 25 minutes to commute, leaving the house 26 minutes before your arrival time is not a good idea. Listen to the weather report the night before. If bad weather is predicted, allow extra time in the morning. Listen to the local news in the morning for report of traffic delays, and cut your morning routine short to allow extra time to get to work.
- **If you drive to work, keep your car in good repair.** Dead batteries, empty gas tanks, and flat tires can often be avoided with regular maintenance.
- **If you use public transportation, listen to the morning news or download apps that let you know about delays.** Leave early every morning in case you get no advance notice of delays.

Apply

Case: Everyone Else Is Late

Dusan Petkovic/ Shutterstock.com

You are a friendly and efficient employee. Customers and coworkers like you. You know that you are doing a good job and receive frequent compliments on your performance from customers. You have one big problem. Several of your coworkers are seldom on time. They arrive late—in the morning, after lunch, even returning from breaks. You feel they are taking advantage of your high level of productivity. Your supervisor, however, does not seem to notice what the other workers are doing. You are tired of covering for them when they are not there.

Case Analysis

1. List three options for dealing with your job situation.

_____

_____

_____

_____

_____

_____

_____

_____

_____

_____

2. List the option you would choose, and explain why you would choose it.

_____

_____

_____

_____

_____

_____

_____

_____

_____

_____

_____

_____

_____

_____

_____

Review

True or False

Indicate *T* if the statement is true or *F* if the statement is false.

1. _____Employees who are late several days a week are usually put on flextime.

2. _____Tardiness and absenteeism reduce employees' productivity.

3. _____One worker's absence or tardiness affects other workers.

4. _____Managers overlook absenteeism and tardiness if the worker is good at the job.

5. _____All businesses have written guidelines on vacation time and tardiness.

6. _____Emergency absences are expected by employers.

7. _____It is unprofessional to often be late to work.

8. _____Employers need to understand that a busy life and hectic weekend often leave workers exhausted and unable to get to work on time on Monday morning.

9. _____When workers have good attendance records, managers notice it whether or not they ever mention it.

10. _____It is as important to return to work on time after breaks as it is to arrive on time in the morning.

Check Your Understanding

1. How can absenteeism and tardiness interfere with the success of a business?

_____

_____

_____

_____

_____

_____

_____

_____

2. How can absenteeism and tardiness interfere with a worker's success?

_____

_____

_____

_____

_____

_____

_____

3. List six ways you can avoid tardiness.

_____

_____

_____

_____

_____

_____

_____

_____

_____

_____

_____

_____

Journal Writing

1. What methods do you use to avoid being late to school, work, or other activities? Do these methods work? If not, what could you do to improve?

_____
_____
_____
_____
_____
_____
_____
_____
_____
_____
_____
_____
_____
_____
_____
_____

2. Do you consider yourself to be a reliable person? Explain by providing examples of your reliability.

_____
_____
_____
_____
_____
_____
_____
_____
_____
_____
_____
_____
_____
_____
_____
_____
_____

17 Career Plateaus

Objectives

- Understand causes of career plateaus.
- Develop strategies for coping with career plateaus.

Key Terms

career plateau

career path

The desire to get ahead and excel in your career motivates you to do your best.

Case

Changes in the Workplace

Riley has just marked his third year with CT, a company that installs business computer systems. Riley started working at CT right after graduation from college. He learned the business quickly and is very good at his job. He has received good reviews, two pay raises, and more responsibility. Riley has high hopes for moving ahead in his career.

Recently, Riley was made project leader on a big contract for an online retail company. The project went very well, and the client's sales increased because of Riley's work. Riley got a large bonus. His boss, Yesenia, promised him more chances to be a project leader. "You are doing an excellent job," she said. "You could be promoted to project manager within a year." Riley appreciated the praise. "Nothing can stop me now," he thought.

Within a few months, though, the president of CT announced that the company was up for sale. A large firm bought CT, and things began to change. The large firm is most interested in CT's expertise in servicing already installed systems. The newly combined company will no longer work with online technology.

At first, Riley remained a productive member of the programming department. However, he became bored working with installed systems. He missed the excitement of developing new programs. His ability to create systems for new online technology is no longer what the company needs.

Although Riley received an annual raise, it was much less than before. Yesenia tells him to focus on managing people. "Go back to college and get a master's in business administration. Now that you are part of a big company, that's how to get ahead," she says. However, Riley does not really want to manage people; he wants to work with new technology.

As time goes on, Riley becomes more and more discouraged. He can see his career is going nowhere. "It just isn't fair," he tells Yesenia. "I'm losing my chance to grow. I've used up three years of my life in this company, and nobody cares."

Riley's disappointment and negative attitude become obvious to his coworkers and to Yesenia. It takes him days to do the amount of work he used to do in hours. He takes long lunches and browses the internet looking for interesting positions with other companies. The others in his department have to work harder to pick up the slack.

When one of Riley's coworkers suggests joining a class in advanced programming, Riley says, "What's the use?" This becomes Riley's standard reply to any suggestions to enhance his skills.

Case Analysis

After you have read the case *Changes in the Workplace*, answer the
following questions.

1. What caused the change in Riley's situation?

_____

_____

_____

2. What could Riley do to improve his situation?

_____

_____

_____

3. What mistakes did Riley make?

_____

_____

_____

4. What caused the change in Riley's attitude?

_____

_____

_____

5. Describe how Riley could have responded in a more positive way.

_____

_____

_____

6. What might happen to Riley if he does not change his attitude?

_____

_____

_____

_____

7. What advice would you give to Riley?

_____

_____

_____

_____

Analyze

Most people begin their careers full of high hopes and ambition. The desire to get ahead and excel in your career motivates you to do your best. Your attitude is positive and constructive. You feel successful when your efforts are rewarded with more responsibility, raises, and promotions. Setting goals and working to achieve them increases your chances for career success.

When things are going well, it's natural to assume that the trend will continue. If you begin climbing the ladder of success, you may expect that your progress will be steady. If the situation changes, you might be thrown off course. Coping with the ups and downs of a career can be a challenge. Finding ways to stay focused and positive are essential to your career success.

Plateaus Are Normal

In the real world, progress toward your career goal may be stalled at times. In geography, a plateau is a flat area of land that is higher than the surrounding land. A **career plateau** is a period in your career when you feel like you are unable to make progress. Plateaus can last from several months to several years. Most people experience one or more plateau periods while pursuing their career goals.

There can be many reasons for a career plateau. If you are doing your job well and your career seems to be on track, the plateau is probably due to outside forces. You may be in a company where there are few openings in positions above yours. You may be in the wrong job. If you do not like your work or are not performing well, you are not likely to make progress. Riley reached a career plateau when his company was sold. When a company changes structure or direction, workers' career goals are often affected.

Keep in mind that many people reach a certain level in their careers and are very happy. They do not wish to rise any further. They have reached their career goals. What might seem like a plateau to one person is the top of the mountain for someone else.

Coping with a Career Plateau

A career plateau will naturally bring feelings of frustration and unhappiness. If something changes in your work responsibilities or your chances for promotion, you might feel bored and unfulfilled. If you feel the plateau is a result of decisions you made, your self-confidence may take a dive.

Keeping a positive attitude is difficult, but it is essential to career advancement. If you can maintain that positive attitude in a frustrating situation, your constructive efforts will be rewarded. If you need to find a new position, a positive attitude will propel your job search. If you need to stay where you are, your positive attitude will be noticed and appreciated by coworkers and supervisors.

How did Riley react to the frustration of his career plans? His attitude became negative and destructive. His productivity fell. His coworkers may eventually resent having to pick up the slack. His boss will also notice the fall in his productivity and his change in attitude. She will no longer see him as having leadership qualities, and his chances for advancement will fall. The key to weathering a plateau is to stay positive. The following strategies can help.

Talk with Your Manager

Even if there is no way to change the immediate situation, talk with your manager about your career goals. You may receive reassurance that the plateau will be short; you may not. In either case, your desire to advance will be on record.

When you speak with your manager, make sure you do not come across as complaining. If you are offered constructive suggestions, agree to think about them. Do not make negative comments about others, even if you feel that someone else is getting in your way of progress. Maintaining good relationships is important to your future ability to move beyond the plateau.

Continue Your Education

A job that is not making full use of your abilities can leave you feeling drained if you are bored and unchallenged. On the positive side, however, it can leave you with leftover energy to apply to your future plans. Use the energy to polish your skills or learn new ones. Getting training to improve your skills or learning a new skill may help you get out of a plateau period.

Be Active and Visible

Do not withdraw because you are unhappy. Speak up at meetings. Offer to train a new employee. Join in company activities such as the softball team or a fundraising event. Serve on the planning committee for the annual holiday party. Write an article for the employee newsletter. Being active in these ways will help you stay connected and open to future opportunities. You might also meet new colleagues who can help you get ahead.

Accept Challenges

Do not turn down new assignments. Do not get stuck doing only what you like or what you feel you do best. There may be several ways to reach your career goal. How you move from one job to another to reach your goal is called a career path. The best career path for getting ahead may not be the one that moves you straight up from one level to another. If a different career path presents itself, seriously consider pursuing it. You might find that it takes you closer to your goal than expected.

Consider a Job Change

Consider all your options with your current employer before deciding to look outside for a new job. If you are sure those options are limited or will take too long to materialize, it may be a good time to consider moving on. For Riley, his current company is not the company he joined three years ago. The focus of CT's business changed with the sale of the company. Riley should consider looking for a job with a company that needs his skills and experience.

When you decide to leave a job, continue to do your very best until you actually leave. You may have to work with that organization or some of its employees in the future.

ESB Professional/Shutterstock.com

hdoeljindoel/
Shutterstock.com

Apply

Case: Stuck on a Plateau

You have been working at your job for two years. The first year you received a raise and a promise of more responsibility if you kept up the good work. Now another year has gone by, and you are unhappy with your progress. You have not received a raise, and there has been no talk of promotion. When you ask about taking a training course to learn new skills, you are told there is not enough money in the budget this year. You have been a solid performer and have proven your loyalty to the company. Now you are beginning to question why you are not making the progress you had expected.

Case Discussion

1. List three options for dealing with your job situation.

_____
_____
_____
_____
_____
_____
_____
_____
_____
_____

2. List the option you would choose, and explain why you would choose it.

_____
_____
_____
_____
_____
_____
_____
_____
_____
_____
_____
_____
_____
_____

Review

True or False

Indicate *T* if the statement is true or *F* if the statement is false.

1. _____ There is nothing wrong with reaching a certain level in your career and being happy to stay there.

2. _____ Highly productive employees almost never hit plateaus as they advance.

3. _____ Most workers reach their career goals without experiencing plateau periods.

4. _____ Plateau periods are most often caused by an individual's action or inaction.

5. _____ Maintaining a positive attitude during a plateau is almost impossible, and employers and coworkers understand this.

6. _____ What seems like a plateau to some people is the top of the mountain to others.

7. _____ A worker should discuss it with the supervisor when hitting a plateau.

8. _____ Plateau periods are the perfect time to relax and take it easy at work.

9. _____ There is no good reason to volunteer for new assignments if the reasons for the plateau are beyond your control.

10. _____ When you reach a plateau, it is usually best to start looking for a new job right away.

Check Your Understanding

1. Why is it important to maintain a positive attitude during a plateau period?

_____

_____

_____

_____

_____

_____

_____

2. What actions by a worker might cause a career plateau?

_____

_____

_____

_____

_____

_____

_____

_____

3. What are some outside forces that might cause a career plateau?

_____

_____

_____

_____

_____

_____

_____

_____

4. List five suggestions for how to stay positive during a career plateau.

_____

_____

_____

_____

_____

_____

_____

_____

Journal Writing

Have you ever hit a plateau when you expected to continue progressing? Describe the plateau. How did it develop? How long did it last? How did you feel? Did you do something to end the plateau? How did this experience affect your attitude toward future involvement in that endeavor?

_____

_____

_____

_____

_____

_____

_____

_____

_____

_____

_____

_____

_____

_____

_____

_____

_____

_____

_____

_____

_____

_____

_____

_____

_____

_____

_____

_____

_____

_____

_____

_____

18 Career Progress

Objectives

- Set goals to help you advance in your career.
- Learn strategies to help you achieve your career goals.

Key Terms

ambition
career goal
mentor
professional organizations
networking

Define your goal, then develop a plan to reach it.

Jacob Lund/Shutterstock.com

Case

Working Smart

Gabriella is a video technician in the news department of a local broadcasting company. The job uses all the skills she learned in school. She also works with experienced video editors who are teaching her new skills.

The pace in the newsroom is very fast, but Gabriella keeps up. She is friendly and efficient. Her coworkers and supervisor like her.

Gabriella has goals beyond video editing. She wants to be a news editor and then a news director. Gabriella knows it is possible because Sharona has done just that. Gabriella asks Sharona, the assistant director of news operations, to lunch to get advice. "I heard you started in the video editing room, but quickly moved on. I want to be like you," Gabriella says.

Sharona advises, "The video editing department is used by several shows at the station. Each show likes to have its work done in a certain way. Get to know what each one wants, so you can do flawless work for every show."

Gabriella takes Sharona's advice and works on learning about other shows and departments in the company. Sharona introduces her to the department heads and directors. She watches all the station's programs and is able to greet directors and producers by name and mention their shows.

Gabriella also keeps her focus on the job she has. She organizes her files of footage and labels them. This way, when footage from a previous broadcast is needed, Gabriella can find it quickly. The department head, Greg, notices what a timesaver her filing system is.

"Gabriella, how would you like to set up a system for the whole department?" Greg asks. Gabriella gladly agrees. Greg mentions her excellent work and creativity to others, and she is given more demanding jobs. She enjoys the challenges.

One day there is a breaking story of an out-of-control fire. Sharona asks for Gabriella to be assigned to her team. They work overtime to prepare footage for the breaking story and a news special. Gabriella never complains or seems tired, even though they work late into the night. She pitches in and does whatever is needed. Gabriella is not afraid to speak up. She offers suggestions and ideas without being pushy. She is able to explain herself clearly and thoughtfully. Gabriella reminds Sharona of herself ten years ago.

When a job for a newsroom video supervisor opens, Sharona recommends Gabriella. After posting the job and interviewing several candidates, the director decides that Gabriella is the most qualified. When Gabriella is offered the job, she happily accepts.

Case Analysis

After you have read the case *Working Smart*, answer the following questions.

1. What is Gabriella's attitude toward her job?

_____

_____

2. What is Gabriella's goal?

_____

_____

3. What does Gabriella do to reach her goal?

_____

_____

4. Do you think Gabriella will reach her goal? Why or why not?

_____

_____

_____

_____

5. What role did Sharona play in Gabriella's career plans?

_____

_____

_____

6. What did Gabriella do to show her desire to move ahead?

_____

_____

_____

7. What did Gabriella do to show her initiative?

_____

_____

8. What did Gabriella do to show her work ethic?

_____

_____

_____

_____

Analyze

For some people, finding a good job is their goal. Once they have found the right job, they are happy and productive. Their goal is to stay there and be the best they can be. Deciding not to change jobs or take on more responsibility may be a choice that leaves room for other interests or family time. Whatever the reason, there is nothing wrong with finding a job that suits you and staying there.

Others, however, are driven by ambition, the desire for rank, fame, money, power, or a combination of these things. They want to move onward and upward. Ambitious people want new challenges and responsibilities. Generally, the rewards are higher status and higher pay. The responsibilities they seek may include challenges, from difficult situations and harder work to more stress and risk of failure.

Have Clear Career Goals

For ambitious people, the rewards are worth the challenges. For those who want to move up in their careers, there are certain steps that help in achieving career goals. A career goal is a clearly defined objective that identifies the specific job or career path a person wishes to achieve.

When you are in a job and know you want to advance, define your goal, then develop a plan to reach it. Gabriella enjoyed her job as a video editor. As she became more familiar with the company, she identified her long-term goal: to become a news director. Once she identified this specific goal, she could start taking steps to reach it.

If you are having trouble determining your career goal, talk with your supervisor or human resources director. Look at online job sites to understand the position titles and experience required to get where you want to go. Seek advice from people who have moved ahead in their careers, both within and outside of your field.

Identify Realistic Steps

Gabriella identified the first step on her path to news director. She needed to be promoted to supervisor in the video editing department. To put herself in a position for promotion, Gabriella needed to demonstrate several things: her technical and creative skills, her initiative, and her strong work ethic. She demonstrated her skills by keeping up with the fast pace of her job. She worked hard to turn in flawless work. She showed initiative by developing a way to organize files that impressed the department head. Because Gabriella worked hard and worked smart, she was given more demanding tasks.

Find a Mentor

Gabriella also looked for a mentor in the company. A **mentor** is a person with experience who supports and advises someone with less experience to help them develop. Gabriella had heard about and observed Sharona, a person who had achieved career growth in the company. She reached out to Sharona and learned about her career path. Sharona helped Gabriella make contacts by introducing her to important people. Once Gabriella had shown her good job skills combined with good human relations skills, Sharona gave her an opportunity to move ahead.

Whether or not you find a strong mentor like Sharona, it is important to develop positive relationships with coworkers and supervisors. Relationships are an important element in career advancement. Gabriella would not have developed a reputation as an outstanding worker if she had only focused on her job skills. It was the combination of good job skills and human relations skills, a constructive work attitude, and the influence of a mentor that assured her success.

Show Initiative

Take every opportunity to show initiative. Volunteer for challenging tasks. Suggest changes to improve efficiency or morale in your department.

Gabriella took it upon herself to reorganize the filing system for the video footage. The department head noticed that her new system made it easier to find footage. He asked her to share it with the department. By doing so, she helped her coworkers become more productive. Gabriella earned their respect and that of her supervisor. At the same time, she increased her visibility and drew positive attention to herself and her skills.

Know Your Organization

Learn as much as you can about the organization you work for. Know the products or services it offers and what each department does. Learn how your company is structured. Who are the department heads? Who does the hiring, firing, and promoting? Are people usually promoted from within the company or brought in from outside when an opening develops? Your chances to advance are greatest in a company that promotes from within.

Know Your Field

Keep up with the latest news and developments in your field. Read articles and attend events to meet people and learn more. We live in a society where change takes place rapidly. Keeping up with trends, influential people, and events in your field gives you food for conversation with people on the job. Being aware of developments in your field is one way to let people know you are interested in moving up.

Join the professional organization in your field and be active. **Professional organizations** are groups established to help people be successful in their chosen profession. Their websites and social media provide a wealth of information, and many offer continuing education opportunities. In addition to the educational value, look for events that offer opportunities to meet influential people in your field. This is called **networking**, a means of connecting with people and establishing relationships that help you achieve your career goals.

Be Open to Opportunities

Be receptive to changes and opportunities. Gabriella was lucky to get an offer in the news department, where she wanted to go. What if she had been offered the video supervisor job in a different department? She would have been wise to take it. Opportunities do not always come exactly where or when you want them. When there is an opportunity for you to be promoted into a job that will help you grow and learn new skills, do not be afraid to take a chance. Look for opportunities to prove your ability.

Show Your Ambition

Let people around you see your desire to succeed. You do not have to be pushy or brag. Just show others by your actions that you have ambition. If your goal is a management position, prepare now. Take courses in management and employee relations. Dress like a manager. Volunteer to lead projects. Offer to head a committee to solve a problem or develop a new procedure. Be willing to take the jobs that no one else wants. Become involved in your company's charitable efforts and special events. You may learn the most from the difficult projects.

Keep Your Attitude Positive

As you achieve your goals, do not leave your positive attitude behind. Good human relations skills are important no matter how high you go in an organization. Often, the higher you go, the more important relationships become.

Conduct yourself so that when your promotion is announced, others will be happy for you. Do not ever indulge in putting others down to get ahead. This type of behavior will damage your reputation. If you feel it is necessary to behave this way, perhaps it is time to think again about your goals.

When you are promoted, do all you can to make the transition smooth. Leave your work in order. Volunteer to train the person who will be taking over your present job. If that is not possible, leave written information about the job. Include your new phone number, and let your replacement and supervisor know that you will be happy to answer any questions they have.

Jacob Lund/
Shutterstock.com

Apply

Case: Promoted over Your Friends

You are the lead project manager in your department. Because you are happy to help your coworkers, your excellent record is not resented but respected. You look forward to going to work every day. You genuinely like the people you work with. You often socialize with them after work and on weekends. In fact, you consider two of your coworkers your best friends.

The day after your supervisor announces a transfer to another city, you are offered the promotion. Although being a manager is your next career goal, you did not think it would happen in this department. Your supervisor is very young, and you did not expect the position to be open anytime soon. Now you are worried—how can you ever be an authority figure to your friends?

Case Analysis

1. List three options for dealing with your job situation.

_____
_____
_____
_____
_____
_____
_____
_____
_____
_____

2. List the option you would choose, and explain why you would choose it.

_____
_____
_____
_____
_____
_____
_____
_____
_____
_____

Review

True or False

Indicate *T* if the statement is true or *F* if the statement is false.

1. _____Everyone has to have ambition for career success.
2. _____The first step in career advancement is to define your goals.
3. _____Goals that require numerous steps to achieve are not worth the effort.
4. _____A mentor is someone who promotes you over other people if they like you.
5. _____It is best not to let others see that you have a desire to get ahead.
6. _____Sharing good ideas that increase group productivity is a good way to show initiative.
7. _____If you want to be a manager, taking courses and dressing like a manager are good strategies.
8. _____Professional organizations are only good for reading articles in your field.
9. _____The desire to have a position of power or high rank is something you should try to hide.
10. _____When people are promoted, they should volunteer to train their replacement.

Check Your Understanding

1. Do you have to be ambitious to achieve work success? Explain your answer.

_____

_____

_____

_____

_____

_____

_____

_____

_____

2. List the strategies that will help you achieve career success.

_____

_____

_____

_____

_____

_____

_____

_____

3. How can a worker determine the best way to advance?

_____

_____

_____

_____

_____

_____

_____

_____

_____

_____

_____

_____

_____

_____

_____

Journal Writing

1. Are you ambitious? What actions or thoughts support your answer?

_____
_____
_____
_____
_____
_____
_____
_____
_____
_____
_____

2. Describe the type of career you want. Why do you think it suits your abilities, interests, and personality?

_____
_____
_____
_____
_____
_____
_____
_____
_____
_____
_____

3. List the five career strategies that are best suited to your ambition and your way of working. Explain your reason for selecting each one.

_____
_____
_____
_____
_____
_____
_____
_____
_____
_____
_____

PART 4
Dealing with Problems on the Job

stokkete/Shutterstock.com

19 Learning from Mistakes

Objectives

- Have the ability to admit making mistakes.
- Learn strategies for dealing with mistakes.

Key Term

perfectionist

If you are afraid to try something new, you limit your opportunities for growth.

fizkes/Shutterstock.com

Case

Budget Blues

Business at the Vegan Food Shop is booming. Amir started working as a delivery person when he was in high school. Back then, the company had only five employees. When Amir graduated, he began working for the company full-time.

Today, there are 20 full-time workers in the shipping department alone, and Amir is the assistant manager. The owner, Hannah, admires his hard work and enthusiasm. He has been with her as the business grew from local to regional, and now it is expanding to ship nationally.

With Hannah's encouragement, Amir is attending college at night, majoring in business administration. Amir owes Hannah a lot. She has helped him move ahead in the company and has given him chances to try new things. When Amir was hesitant, Hannah pushed him. "Test yourself, Amir," she always says. "I have confidence in you. You just need confidence in yourself."

Amir hates to make a mistake; but he does make some. Hannah never yells at him, even when he mailed a shipment to Portland, Maine, instead of Portland, Oregon. Her attitude is that mistakes happen. She is satisfied as long as you do your best, take steps to prevent mistakes, and correct those that happen. Her attitude makes it easier for Amir to admit when he is wrong. Overcoming his fear of failure has helped him gain the confidence to take on new assignments.

One Monday afternoon, Hannah calls Amir to her office and tells him that she is swamped with work. She must report on the cost of the expansion for the Friday meeting. "I've already calculated the staffing needs," she tells him, "but I need to prepare budgets for the cost of running your department, and I have to be in Texas tomorrow for that conference. I wish I could send you to Texas to speak in my place."

"Thanks for the vote of confidence, but I certainly don't have enough experience to speak in your place. However, I can finish the report for you. I know I can do it."

"Amir, this time I'm not so sure. You've never done budgets before. The decision to expand will be made at Friday's meeting, based on my report. However, I have no choice. You've done well in other areas. Give it your best."

Amir begins the report Tuesday morning. He works steadily, and the budget is on Hannah's desk by Wednesday evening.

Thursday morning, Hannah calls Amir to her office. Expecting a pat on the back, Amir is amazed to hear her say, "I'm afraid the figures you used to estimate mailing costs are outdated. You didn't factor in the potential postage increases."

Amir feels dizzy. "Oh, no! I didn't know I was supposed to do that. I'd like the chance to correct my mistake."

"Well, it's a good thing you got this done a day early," Hannah said. "This mistake would have made management lose all confidence in me. I know it was just an oversight. The rest of the report looks excellent. Have the revised figures on my desk this afternoon."

Case Analysis

After you have read the case *Budget Blues*, answer the following questions.

1. What do you think about the way Hannah responded to Amir's mistake?

_____

_____

2. What do you think about the way Amir responded when Hannah pointed out his mistake?

_____

_____

3. What is the best way to respond when you find out that you have made a mistake?

_____

_____

_____

4. Why do you think Amir made the mistake in the report?

_____

_____

5. Did Hannah make a mistake in trusting Amir to do the report correctly? Explain your answer.

_____

_____

_____

6. What do you think Amir learned from this mistake?

_____

_____

7. What effect do you think this mistake will have on Amir's relationship with Hannah?

_____

_____

_____

8. What effect do you think this mistake will have on Amir's future?

_____

_____

_____

Analyze

The more you do, the more opportunities you have to make mistakes. The only people who make *no* mistakes are those who will never admit their mistakes. They always find a way to blame something or someone else. They are not fooling anyone. Everyone makes mistakes.

Admit It, No Excuses

Mistakes come in all sizes. Big mistakes are often embarrassing, and in the workplace they can be costly. However, once you make a mistake, big or small, take responsibility. Then, correct it if possible, and put it behind you.

Do not make excuses for your mistakes or try to cover them up. Covering up a mistake can lead to more problems than the original mistake itself. If you are caught trying to cover up a mistake, you appear to be dishonest as well as careless. Fiorello LaGuardia was one of the most popular and effective mayors of New York City. He once said, "When I make a mistake, it's a beaut!" The voters liked him for his honesty.

Amir made a mistake that could have been costly. To his credit, he admitted it immediately. He did not make excuses or attempt to blame a third party. He quickly apologized and offered to correct his error. His reaction confirmed Hannah's confidence in him. His self-confidence was shaken, but correcting his error promptly helped restore confidence in himself.

Do Not Fear Making Mistakes

Fear of making mistakes can cause you to avoid risks and prevent you from taking action. If you are afraid to try something new, you limit your opportunities for growth. Hannah took a chance on Amir; Amir took a chance on himself.

The outcome was that Amir stretched his abilities and accomplished something he had never tried before. Because of his ability and willingness to fix his mistake, Hannah is more likely to offer Amir new assignments. He will continue advancing in his career.

If you are a **perfectionist**, you are someone who wants to do everything perfectly and dreads making a mistake. Fear of making a mistake can cause you to pass up opportunities that could advance your career. Do not avoid new challenges out of fear. The decision to refuse an opportunity because you fear failure is the mistake you should avoid making.

Realize that it is not possible to do a perfect job all the time. Always do the best you can, but be realistic. Remind yourself that most mistakes can be corrected. If a decision to take on new challenges doesn't work out, be positive and use what you have learned to go forward.

Learn from Mistakes

The ability to learn from mistakes can make the difference between success and failure. View your mistakes as opportunities to learn and improve. Then you will most likely reach your goals. If you make a career move that doesn't work out, look at failure as a stepping stone to success. Many of today's most successful entrepreneurs were unsuccessful in their first, second, third, or even fourth attempts at building a business. Rather than let these failures get them down, they took the knowledge they gained from failing and used it to achieve success. Follow the wise words of this famous saying, "If at first you don't succeed, try, try again."

CREATISTA/Shutterstock.com

Apply

Case: Oops!

*Amnaj Khetsamtip/
Shutterstock.com*

As you are leaving work on Friday evening, your supervisor's phone rings. Since everyone else has left, you answer. It is an important message from the firm's largest customer. A problem has come up, and your supervisor needs to bring additional information to the Monday morning meeting. You write the information on your phone message pad and head home.

On Monday morning, you arrive at work bright and early. You get right to work on an important project. Suddenly, you look at your message pad. "Oh, no!" you say out loud. You forgot to give the message to your supervisor, and she is already on her way to the meeting.

Case Analysis

1. List three options for dealing with your job situation.

_____

_____

_____

_____

_____

_____

_____

_____

_____

_____

2. List the option you would choose, and explain why you would choose it.

_____

_____

_____

_____

_____

_____

_____

_____

_____

_____

_____

_____

_____

_____

Review

True or False

Indicate *T* if the statement is true or *F* if the statement is false.

1. _____ People who are perfectionists never make mistakes.

2. _____ Once a person fails at something, the mistake will most likely ruin their career.

3. _____ Covering up a mistake can make a person appear to be dishonest.

4. _____ Fear of making mistakes can limit a person's opportunity for growth.

5. _____ A perfectionist is a person who dreads making a mistake.

6. _____ Mistakes can be opportunities to learn and grow as a professional.

7. _____ When a worker makes a mistake, the best thing to do is admit it and work to fix it as soon as possible.

8. _____ A person with a constructive attitude looks for opportunities to cover up mistakes.

9. _____ People with successful businesses became successful because they never made any mistakes.

10. _____ Refusing an opportunity because you fear failure is itself a big mistake.

Check Your Understanding

1. Describe how making mistakes can help your career.

_____
_____
_____
_____
_____
_____
_____
_____
_____
_____
_____

2. Describe the advantages and disadvantages of being a perfectionist.

_____
_____
_____
_____
_____
_____
_____
_____
_____
_____
_____

3. Imagine that a coworker has made a mistake. What advice would you give?

_____
_____
_____
_____
_____
_____
_____
_____
_____
_____
_____

Journal Writing

Describe a mistake you made recently. What lesson did you learn from the experience?

_____

_____

_____

_____

_____

_____

_____

_____

_____

_____

_____

_____

_____

_____

_____

_____

_____

_____

_____

_____

_____

_____

_____

_____

_____

_____

_____

_____

_____

_____

_____

_____

_____

How Do You Handle Mistakes?

Everyone makes mistakes. When you make a mistake, the best thing to do is admit it. Correct the mistake as soon as possible, and then determine what you need to do to keep from making the same mistake again. Answer the following questions based on your own experience.

1. Think of a mistake you made that you had to correct.

_____
_____
_____

2. How did you feel when you realized you made this mistake?

_____
_____
_____

3. Did you admit your mistake promptly? If yes, did it help? If not, did it make matters worse?

_____
_____
_____

4. Why do you think you made this mistake?

_____
_____
_____

5. What did you learn from this mistake?

_____
_____
_____

6. Did you use this mistake as a learning experience or a stepping stone to new achievements? Explain.

_____
_____

7. Has fear of making a mistake ever prevented you from doing something? Explain.

_____
_____
_____

8. If fear of making a mistake has kept you from doing something, what could you do to overcome this fear?

_____
_____

20 Repairing Relationships

Objectives

- Recognize the causes of damaged relationships.
- Understand how to avoid damaging relationships.
- List effective strategies to repair damaged relationships.

Key Terms

misunderstanding
miscommunication
competition
common courtesy
rapport
personality conflict
mutually rewarding relationship

Act promptly to restore damaged relationships.

MBI/Shutterstock.com

Case

Where's Your Sense of Humor?

Jennifer and Lynnette are legal assistants in a large law firm. Jennifer is new and wants to make a good impression on all the attorneys in the office. On a Friday morning, John Humphrey, one of the top attorneys, calls Jennifer into his office and hands her a huge box of contracts and other legal papers. "Look, I know it's short notice, but I need all of this stuff sorted, alphabetized, and placed in individual folders by noon. I have to be in court by one o'clock, and I need to take all of this with me."

Jennifer was stunned. It was a huge amount of work, and she would have to do it alone. This was the day that Lynnette was attending a computer training course. "You need all of this?" she asked. "Are you sure?"

John smiled. "Positive. If it's not all ready, I'll lose my case before it even gets started. I know you don't want that to happen."

"Of course not," Jennifer felt a lump of fear rise in her throat—she couldn't possibly finish all of this, but what would happen if she didn't?

At noon, Lynnette returned from the morning session of her course. "Hi, Jennifer," she said cheerily. "Want to grab a quick sandwich in the cafeteria?"

"I can't," Jennifer said. "Look at all this stuff John asked me to sort and file. He needs it in court by one o'clock, and I'm not even halfway done. Can you stay and help me?"

"Let me see what it is," Lynnette took the papers and began leafing through them. "That's strange. This is an old case. John couldn't possibly need these. Are you sure this is what he asked you to do?"

"I'm positive," said Jennifer. "He said he will lose the case if these files aren't ready."

To Jennifer's surprise, Lynnette started to laugh. "I can't believe it!" she exclaimed. "He did the same thing to me when I first started."

"And you think it's funny?"

"Now I do. At the time, I was furious. I forgot to tell you that John loves practical jokes. This is his way of 'breaking in' the new recruits."

"What?" Jennifer couldn't believe it.

Just then John walked out of his office. He looked at Lynnette, and they both screeched with laughter. "You didn't think I was serious, did you?" John continued laughing.

"Of course, I did!" said Jennifer.

"It was a test! I wanted to see if you would remember that trials never start on Friday afternoon," John continued, still chuckling.

"Well, I didn't remember—I haven't been here that long. And I don't think it's funny!"

Jennifer burst into tears and ran off to the restroom.

John looked at Lynnette. "Wow, she's really thin-skinned," he said, still chuckling.

"You need to apologize right now," Lynnette gave him a stern look. "You can't afford to lose any more friends around here with your stupid jokes."

"I suppose," John said, shaking his head. "Nobody has a sense of humor anymore."

Case Analysis

After you have read the case *Where's Your Sense of Humor?*, answer the following questions.

1. What is your reaction to this case?

_____

_____

2. Do you think John's joke was "mean" or just for fun?

_____

_____

_____

3. If you were in Jennifer's situation, what would you do?

_____

_____

_____

4. What role did Lynnette play in the situation? Was it positive or negative?

_____

_____

_____

5. What role did company culture play in this case?

_____

_____

_____

6. Will Jennifer and John be able to repair their relationship? Explain your answer.

_____

_____

_____

7. How do you think Lynette and Jennifer will interact after this conflict?

_____

_____

_____

_____

_____

Analyze

You are bound to have some conflicts with people on the job. Whatever the cause, when conflicts occur, the best response is to try to clear the air. To do so, you need to try to understand the other person's reactions and feelings. When Lynnette saw Jennifer's response, she asked John to apologize. If John does not try to repair the damage he has done, nothing will be resolved.

Once John saw that Jennifer was embarrassed and upset, he could have taken a different approach. Instead of laughing, what if he had said, "I'm so sorry, Jennifer. I shouldn't have subjected you to my practical jokes." This response would have made matters better immediately.

A misunderstanding can damage a relationship in the workplace. When conflicts occur, it is not always easy to forgive and forget. Remember, though, that communication is the key to good human relations. If you do not try to talk things through, you are risking permanent damage. In the long run, repairing damaged relationships and soothing ruffled feathers may be more important to your future.

Causes of Damaged Relationships

There are many causes of human relations problems. Conflicts are normal, but they should be resolved promptly. The objective is to avoid permanent damage in relationships.

Problems often arise when behavior causes a misunderstanding, an argument resulting from the failure of two people to understand each other. Your tone, your words, or your body language might be sending the wrong message. In some cases, an attempt at communication goes wrong and results in miscommunication, a failure to communicate adequately and properly. People might not be listening to each other, or they might not be correctly interpreting what the other is saying. Continuing lack of communication can damage relationships.

Competition among coworkers is a common cause of conflict. Competition occurs when two or more people are trying to reach the same goal. It might be a plum project. It could be a promotion. Sometimes it is as simple as trying to get the boss to notice them. When coworkers seek to show the boss that they can excel individually, the competition can lead to conflict.

Lack of common courtesy—polite behavior and good etiquette, such as saying "please" and "thank you"—is another cause of damaged relationships. Your seeming lack of gratitude or being polite can cause a person to feel you are taking them for granted. If the person tells you how they feel, you may think they are being overly sensitive. This can cause a problem.

John's reaction to the fact that Jennifer took his instruction seriously was discourteous. He should have understood that everyone does not appreciate practical jokes when it is at their expense. He should not have pulled the stunt in the first place. When he saw Jennifer's reaction, he should have apologized immediately without being told.

How to Avoid Relationship Problems

Show interest and concern for your coworkers. Be willing to do extra work without complaining. These actions will create good relationships. As a result, if conflicts arise, you will have an easier time working them out.

When you are part of a team, be aware of other team members' needs. Use this awareness to avoid conflict. Let your coworkers know that you care about their feelings. Make a practice of showing good manners.

Even when you know people well, don't take them for granted. If you do not know someone, do not make assumptions about them or how they might respond to something you say or do. Make an effort to establish rapport, a friendly, harmonious relationship that makes communication easy and productive.

How to Repair Damaged Relationships

Resolve to act promptly to restore damaged relationships. Even if you are not responsible for the misunderstanding, take the first steps to repair it.

Permit others to repair relationships with you. Do not give in to hurt feelings or nurse minor conflicts into major problems. Listen to the other person. Jennifer should accept her coworkers' apology and allow the healing process to begin. Eventually, if she grows to like and respect John, she might see the humor in the situation after all, just as Lynnette did.

In your dealings with others, resolve not to leap to conclusions. Do not always look for a negative explanation for another's behavior. Remember— like you, your coworkers and your supervisor cannot always anticipate how others will feel about their actions. Advancement in your career may very well depend on your ability to repair damaged relationships.

The Dangers of Not Acting

Jennifer might have misread John's motives. He took a joke too far, but she might have overacted. Lynnette realized the problem immediately and took steps to resolve it. If John and Lynnette apologize, Jennifer should accept the gesture and move past the situation.

You May Spend Too Much Time Thinking About the Problem

When you have a conflict, you may find yourself replaying the scene over and over in your mind. You start thinking about everything the person has ever said or done. You begin to see innocent behavior as slights or insults. Anger and hurt feelings are likely to continue and might even worsen.

Rely on your positive attitude to find constructive ways to handle your feelings. If you need a follow-up conversation to clear the air, take the initiative to have it. Avoid going over the issue again; focus on agreement to the way forward toward a good relationship.

Damaged Relationships Add Stress

Like a toothache, an unresolved problem doesn't go away on its own. It is on your mind, even when you would rather be thinking of something else. Most jobs have some stressful aspects that can't be changed, such as long hours, a heavy workload, or complex job tasks. Being angry or having someone else angry with you is a distraction that adds to stress.

Damaged Relationships Can Affect Your Productivity

Dwelling on a problem uses time and energy. Your productivity will start to slip. Often, when conflicts between employees arise, supervisors do not know whom to fault. They are likely to spread the blame evenly. These types of problems are often labeled as a **personality conflict**, discord between people caused by their different temperaments. Even though the conflict starts over a work issue, the lack of a solution is viewed as a personality problem. If you become known as a person who is involved in such a conflict, it can affect your overall performance rating. Employers expect mature people to resolve conflict and not let it affect their work.

Damaged Relationships Can Negatively Impact Your Career

It is possible to become a victim of a conflict. Imagine what damage John could cause Jennifer if she stays angry. In the future, John might dwell on mistakes Jennifer makes. He can avoid giving her projects that give her visibility. He might suggest to other staff members that Jennifer is not a team player. Although John's poor behavior is the cause of the problem, he has a higher rank and can do more damage to Jennifer. The correct move for Jennifer is to forgive and forget and show John that she is a mature professional.

The Value of Good Relationships

You do not have to make close friends at work, but building good relationships is essential to career success. You will learn much more if you have good relationships built on friendliness and trust.

You learned earlier about loyalty and keeping your commitments as the basis for forming good relationships in the workplace. If your career path leads to higher positions, reach back and help others. When your managers and mentors move on, stay in contact with them. Maintaining the relationships you develop over the course of time is a part of networking. When people have a relationship that is beneficial to everyone involved, it is a **mutually rewarding relationship**. Often, the value of these relationships pays off at a point in the future that you could not have predicted.

pixfly/Shutterstock.com

Apply

Case: Angry Words

You are unhappy with a coworker on a joint project. Her work is sloppy, and you have been working late for the past week to fix it. It bothers you that she will get just as much credit as you for the good work on the project. At lunchtime, you discuss your angry feelings with another member of the department. You say some things you immediately regret saying. You hope your angry words are not repeated. Unfortunately, the person you spoke to tells your coworker what you said.

Case Analysis

1. List three options for dealing with your job situation.

_____

_____

_____

_____

_____

_____

_____

_____

_____

_____

2. List the option you would choose, and explain why you would choose it.

_____

_____

_____

_____

_____

_____

_____

_____

_____

_____

_____

_____

_____

_____

Review

True or False

Indicate *T* if the statement is true or *F* if the statement is false.

1. _____Misunderstandings and anger can permanently damage your relationships if allowed to go unrepaired.

2. _____The time spent repairing damaged relationships could be better spent on improving productivity.

3. _____A personality conflict can damage your reputation even if it starts over a legitimate work issue.

4. _____Working with someone who is angry can add to a stressful situation at work.

5. _____Damaged relationships can jeopardize a person's career.

6. _____It is always the supervisor's responsibility to solve conflicts that arise among coworkers.

7. _____Good relationships can pay off in the future in ways you might not anticipate.

8. _____The person who caused the disagreement should always make the first move to heal the relationship.

9. _____A person is allowed to give in to hurt feelings and hold a grudge if not responsible for the misunderstanding.

10. _____Career advancement may depend on a person's ability to repair damaged relationships.

Check Your Understanding

1. List four causes of damaged relationships.

_____

_____

_____

_____

_____

_____

_____

2. List six strategies you can use to repair damaged relationships.

_____

_____

_____

_____

_____

_____

_____

_____

_____

_____

_____

3. Why is it important to repair damaged relationships?

_____

_____

_____

_____

_____

_____

_____

_____

_____

4. Describe the value of good relationships at work.

_____

_____

_____

_____

_____

_____

_____

_____

_____

_____

Journal Writing

Do you think all damaged relationships can be repaired, or are some too damaged to ever return to normal? Explain your answer.

_____
_____
_____
_____
_____
_____
_____
_____
_____
_____
_____
_____
_____
_____
_____
_____
_____
_____
_____
_____
_____
_____
_____
_____
_____
_____
_____
_____
_____
_____
_____
_____
_____
_____
_____
_____

21 Handling Criticism

Objectives

- Learn strategies for handling criticism.
- Understand why constructive criticism can help you succeed.
- Learn how to give constructive criticism.

Key Terms

criticism
defensive
constructive criticism
destructive criticism

Accept criticism and learn from it.

Motortion Films/Shutterstock.com

Case

The Sensitive Artist

Charles has his heart set on attending a famous art academy after completing two years of community college. The cost is very high, but he is convinced that he will be awarded a scholarship. He confidently sends in his application and samples and is stunned when he is rejected.

He calls Mr. Lin, his former art teacher who had encouraged him. "Those big city art snobs," he yells, "they can't even recognize talent when they see it!"

"More training would be good for you, Charles," Mr. Lin responds. "You can use your talent to earn good money. I'm going to call a friend of mine who works for a big architecture firm. He can tell you how to apply for an internship while you finish college."

"I think I'm ready for a regular job if they have openings," says Charles. "Why do I need to start as an intern? I can finish my college degree at night."

Mr. Lin's friend helps Charles apply for a position as an intern in the drafting department. Charles tells his manager, Keisha, "I didn't think I would like this work so much. I always wanted to be an artist."

"I think you do very well with the detail work," Keisha responds. "In a way, it *is* being an artist. You are doing something useful with your talent."

When his internship ends, Charles is hired as a drafter. When there is a review of one of his drawings, Keisha meets with him to discuss it in her office. "Charles," she explains, "we gave you the precise measurements for the window treatments and doorways. Your drawings are off by quite a lot."

"Is that right?" Charles replies, standing up. "Well, I think the client will be happier with what I have proposed. I know what I'm doing, so I think you should adjust your thinking about what the client wants. My proposal is more creative."

"It doesn't work that way in buildings," Keisha replies. "You need to follow the specifications."

Charles walks angrily toward the door. "If they don't appreciate my work around here, maybe I should just reapply to art school. I thought I liked this job, but it's too rigid. I don't need to hear a bunch of complaints."

"No one is complaining," Keisha replies. "You're still learning, and your work is good. You just need to be able to accept criticism and not expect compliments all the time."

Charles continues to feel resentful. He becomes upset whenever he has to make corrections to his work. He feels he is failing in his new job.

Charles begins to resent the architects and senior designers. He feels that they think they are better than he is because they have more education. When one of them questions his placement of any object, he sulks for the rest of the day.

Charles has a great deal of trouble working on a team with other drafters. When his ideas are not used, he is personally insulted. Charles refuses to talk to some coworkers because they have altered his drawings. He is quickly earning a reputation as a troublesome department member.

After Charles has worked as a drafter for 18 months, his boss is forced to cut the staff. Although Charles has more talent than many of the others, he is let go.

Case Analysis

After you have read the case *The Sensitive Artist*, answer the following questions.

1. What is your reaction to this case?

_____

_____

_____

2. How would you describe Charles's attitude toward his job?

_____

_____

3. How would you describe the criticism Charles received?

_____

_____

_____

4. Why was Charles fired?

_____

_____

_____

5. What do you think is the cause of Charles's feelings about criticism?

_____

_____

_____

6. Describe what might have happened if Charles had responded positively to the criticism from his manager.

_____

_____

7. Describe what might have happened if Charles had responded positively to the suggestions from the designers and architects at his job.

_____

_____

_____

8. What advice would you give Charles?

_____

_____

_____

Analyze

Everyone faces criticism at one time or another. Criticism is an expression of disapproval or the act of pointing out problems or faults with something or someone. Criticism might be fair, or it might be unfair. It might come from a source you respect or from someone you do not trust. In the workplace, criticism is to be expected. Being able to accept criticism and to learn from it is an important human relations skill.

Handling Criticism

Criticism hurts. When you do your best, you do not want to be told it is not good enough. Even when you know it is justified, criticism can sting. Many people are not good at delivering criticism. It might be hard for them to sound constructive. At work, your supervisor might wait until review time and give you a list of your mistakes all at once.

To avoid the hurt from criticism, learn how to accept it as a part of life. Do *not* think of criticism as an evaluation of your whole being. One of Charles's mistakes is generalizing criticism of his work to his whole life. When his manager makes suggestions, Charles feels the statements mean his talent is being dismissed. When the designers and architects make suggestions, Charles thinks he is failing in his new job.

A balanced view of yourself can help you handle criticism. Be willing to admit when you are wrong. Develop a "thick skin," and try not to be defensive. Being defensive means refusing to accept responsibility for mistakes and attempting to justify your actions. Instead, you blame others or make excuses. A better response is to listen calmly to criticism and be willing to learn from it.

Here is another approach that is helpful on the job: remember that your goal is to produce the best work for your organization. Suggestions and criticisms are offered to improve the quality of your work. Therefore, you should not take criticism at work personally.

Constructive Criticism Helps You Learn

Criticism can be a learning experience. Constructive criticism is feedback given to help someone improve or learn something. Charles's manager offered him constructive criticism. She wanted to help Charles do his best work. Unfortunately, Charles's defensive attitude prevented him from benefiting from Keisha's feedback. He was unable to accept the constructive advice. Instead, Charles interpreted the criticism as a personal attack. He confused his desire to be judged on his creativity with the need for precision in the kind of work he was hired to do.

Feedback intended to inflict hurt is destructive criticism. Its intention is to wound, not to teach or help. Destructive criticism is often motivated by anger. Imagine how Charles would have felt if his manager had said, "Whatever made you think you were an artist? Look at this dreadful drawing!"

Constructive criticism is not given in anger or as a criticism of you personally. Imagine that Charles's manager criticized his work this way: "Charles, this drawing shows that you have talent. I see you are having a problem with the specifications. Why don't you review the techniques with one of our senior drafters?" Would Charles have responded any differently?

Charles did not understand the difference between constructive and destructive criticism. He was unable to accept criticism and benefit from correcting his mistakes. Ultimately, it cost him his job. Although he has good drafting ability, his negative attitude toward criticism interfered with his relationships and progress at work.

When You Criticize Others

At some point, you may be in the position to give criticism. Perhaps you will be promoted to supervisor. Maybe you will be part of a team that is evaluating a project. Whenever you need to give criticism, make it constructive. Give yourself time to plan what you need to say. Even if you feel angry or upset, do not show it, and do not attack the person. Criticize the work or idea by giving concrete reasons for your feedback. Offer suggestions for improvement. Imagine you are the person you must criticize. Give criticism the way you would like to receive it.

G-Stock Studio/Shutterstock.com

Apply

Case: The New Supervisor

You have been promoted to supervisor. You feel able to handle your new duties. The only problem you are having is with one employee who is not performing well. Rather than doing the most important tasks, the employee does the easiest work and lets the rest sit. The employee is taking long lunch hours and making personal phone calls instead of working. You need to discuss these job performance concerns.

fizkes/Shutterstock.com

Case Discussion

1. List three options for dealing with your job situation.

_____
_____
_____
_____
_____
_____
_____
_____
_____
_____

2. List the option you would choose, and explain why you would choose it.

_____
_____
_____
_____
_____
_____
_____
_____
_____
_____
_____
_____
_____
_____
_____
_____
_____
_____

Review

True or False

Indicate *T* if the statement is true or *F* if the statement is false.

1. _____ Criticism hurts, but it is a part of life.
2. _____ Workers with positive and constructive attitudes escape criticism.
3. _____ Constructive criticism is given to help workers learn and improve.
4. _____ All criticism is constructive.
5. _____ Destructive criticism, although painful, offers suggestions for improving a worker's performance.
6. _____ Criticism should never include a personal attack against another.
7. _____ Criticism given in anger is acceptable if it is justified.
8. _____ Failure to accept constructive criticism can cause a defensive reaction.
9. _____ When you need to give criticism, it is a good idea to plan what you are going to say.
10. _____ The ability to give constructive criticism and avoid giving destructive criticism is an important supervisory skill.

Check Your Understanding

1. Describe constructive criticism.

_____
_____
_____
_____
_____
_____

2. Describe destructive criticism.

_____
_____
_____
_____
_____
_____

3. Why does criticism hurt?

_____
_____
_____
_____
_____
_____

4. How can constructive criticism help you on your job?

_____
_____
_____
_____
_____
_____

5. Give three suggestions for how to give constructive criticism.

_____
_____
_____
_____
_____
_____
_____

Journal Writing

1. Identify a situation in which you received destructive criticism. Describe the situation, the criticism, and your response.

_____

_____

_____

_____

_____

_____

_____

_____

_____

_____

_____

_____

_____

_____

_____

_____

_____

_____

2. Describe a situation in which you received constructive criticism. What did the person say? How did you respond? What was the outcome?

_____

_____

_____

_____

_____

_____

_____

_____

_____

_____

_____

_____

_____

_____

_____

_____

3. Do you know anyone like Charles? Describe the ways in which this person is like Charles. How does this person make you and other people feel? What would you suggest to this person if you were giving constructive criticism?

_____

_____

_____

_____

_____

_____

_____

_____

_____

_____

_____

_____

_____

_____

_____

_____

_____

_____

_____

_____

_____

_____

_____

_____

_____

_____

_____

_____

_____

_____

_____

_____

22 Leaving a Job

Objectives

- Understand how to decide when it is time to leave a job.
- Describe ways to leave a job in a positive manner.
- Explain what to do if you are terminated.

Key Terms

personality conflict
inertia
giving notice
resign
written resignation
terminated
for cause

immediate dismissal
at-will employment
layoff
reduction in force (RIF)
seniority

Deciding when to leave a job is an important step.

Case

Ready to Move On

Austin has worked at a local accounting firm for three years. He majored in accounting in college, and this is his first job. He was hired as a junior accountant. The owners, Jonathan and his wife, Savannah, treat Austin very well. He feels a deep loyalty to them.

During his second year with the firm, Austin decided to take courses at night to become a Certified Public Accountant (CPA). While attending school, Austin received support and encouragement from Jonathan and Savannah. "Work hard and you will succeed, Austin," they told him. "There is a good future for you here."

When Austin passed the CPA exam, his coworkers threw him a surprise party. Soon after, Jonathan and Savannah promoted Austin to senior accountant. Now in his third year with the firm, he is again promoted. His new position is manager of the tax preparation unit. Austin is excited about managing.

Austin joined a professional association, the American Institute of Certified Public Accountants (AICPA). At the meetings, Austin was able to network with people who work for large corporations and accounting firms. He started thinking about what it would be like to work for a large organization. He noticed that people in big firms often have opportunities to travel and some have had the experience of working in other countries. Experiencing the world has always been a dream of Austin's.

Austin does not want to leave just because his firm is not big enough. "Maybe," he thinks, "I can stay and help the firm grow." He asks Jonathan and Savannah about their future plans for the firm. He tells them how they could make it grow. The owners listen intently and praise his initiative. However, they like their firm the way it is. "Small businesses are key to the economic health of our community," says Savannah. "When they succeed, we succeed. We are not interested in large, national accounts."

Jonathan tells Austin they understand his frustration, but adds, "You're young. Be patient, Austin. In a few years, you'll be in a position to become a partner here."

Austin understands and appreciates their outlook, but he knows he is ready to move on. He wants the challenge of working for a large international corporation that offers bigger opportunities.

Austin speaks to a number of his professional colleagues, including Fatima, who works for an international consulting firm. She offers to introduce him to the senior tax advisor in her company.

Austin meets with the tax advisor, who becomes interested in recruiting him for a position. Austin goes through a round of interviews with company executives. The company makes him an offer, and he likes what he hears. Austin prepares to submit his resignation to Jonathan and Savannah as soon as his new job is confirmed in writing.

Case Analysis

After you have read the case *Ready to Move On*, answer the following questions.

1. What is Austin's attitude toward his job?

_____

_____

2. How would you describe Jonathan and Savannah as managers?

_____

_____

_____

3. Do you think Austin made the right decision? Why or why not?

_____

_____

_____

_____

4. What did Austin do to improve his chances of moving up in his career?

_____

_____

_____

5. What did Austin do to explore new job possibilities?

_____

_____

_____

_____

6. Did Fatima give good advice to Austin? Why or why not?

_____

_____

_____

7. What advice would you give to Austin about how to leave his job?

_____

_____

_____

_____

Analyze

How long you stay in a job depends on many factors. How much you enjoy the work, how you feel about the company, and how much you like and respect your coworkers and managers are all factors. Your salary, your opportunities to advance, and your personal life will also play a big part. Deciding when it is time to leave a job is an important step. Leaving a job in a positive manner is equally important.

When Is the Right Time to Leave?

Whether to leave a job is a serious decision. Here are some clues that indicate that you should start thinking about leaving:

- You dread going to work.
- You do not feel valued.
- Your productivity is falling.
- You have received a negative performance review.
- You have been passed over for a promotion.
- Your work is boring.
- There are no opportunities to advance your career.
- Changes take place in the organization that negatively impact you.

If you experience any of the above, it does *not* mean that you should automatically start looking for a new job. It *does* mean that you should examine the reasons and look for solutions, either at your current workplace or outside of it.

Analyze Your Reasons

If you dread going to work because of people around you, try to resolve the problem. It is rarely a good idea to leave a job because of a personality conflict. A **personality conflict** is discord between people caused by their different temperaments. Try to handle the problem in a constructive way without the involvement of your supervisor.

If the problem stems from a destructive attitude on your part, changing jobs might not help. Your negative attitude will travel with you unless it is directly related to your specific work situation. Confront the reasons for your negative attitude and work to correct them. This might be by staying or leaving. You may need advice from trusted friends or colleagues to reach the best decision.

Suppose you are having trouble focusing on your work, your productivity is falling, and you received a negative performance review. Ask yourself, "Am I having personal, family, financial, or other problems outside of work?" Such problems could be causing your poor performance. If these problems are not solved, you are likely to take them with you to your next job. It might be better to stay at your current job and get help to solve your problem. Many companies provide resources to help workers with personal problems.

If you are bored, consult your supervisor or human resources department. Perhaps you can get special training or be placed on a special project. There may be another job in the company that would be more challenging. Austin went back to school for his CPA. Soon after, he was promoted to senior accountant.

If you want to move up, discuss it with your supervisor or human resources department. You may discover opportunities that you did not know existed. If you discover that there is no way for you to advance, then consider looking for a new job.

Make the Decision

Changing jobs is not easy. Your timing and your reasons need to align in a way that makes you feel you know the right thing to do. This is a good time to not be a perfectionist. No job is perfect, and your decision might not feel perfect when you decide whether or not to make a change. When your current job is safe and familiar, you might become too comfortable. You might experience inertia, which means lacking motivation to make changes. Some people stay in jobs because of inertia or fear of the unknown. They are happy enough and see no reason to change. For some people, the safe decision may be the best decision. There is no shame in staying in a job where you are reasonably happy and reasonably productive. However, if you are unhappy and unmotivated, then it might be time to think about making a change.

If Austin decides to stay because of a sense of gratitude, loyalty, or desire for a familiar and comfortable job, it would most likely be a mistake. Eventually, his dissatisfaction and frustration might undermine his positive attitude toward his job. If that begins to happen and he still stays, his productivity might fall and his relationships with his coworkers may deteriorate. It was time for him to move on, and he made the right decision.

In some careers, you are expected to make many job changes. Employers realize that you learn new things with each new job. If you are in one of these careers and want to advance, you will have to accept the risks that come with changing jobs. You will need to weigh the pros and cons and make the decision that is the best for your career goals and your personal happiness.

Leave in a Positive Way

Once you have made the decision to leave, stay positive. Keep your productivity level high even while job hunting. Your present employer is still your first priority.

Do not use any of your current employer's resources for your job hunt. Do not use time at work, the computer, company letterhead or envelopes, the phone, or mailing services.

When you have accepted a new job, you must give notice. Giving notice means telling your supervisor that you intend to resign, which means you are voluntarily leaving your position. The first step is to meet with your supervisor to explain that you are leaving and why. You should also submit a written resignation to your supervisor. A **written resignation** states your intention to leave the job and gives the date of your last day of employment. A typical time for notice of resignation is two to four weeks.

When your intention to leave becomes known, be positive about your reasons for leaving. Resist the urge to make negative comments about any situation that is prompting you to leave. Also, avoid saying anything negative about your coworkers, supervisor, or the company. Leave on a positive note and you will keep all your future options open. You may cross paths with these coworkers in the future. Some day you may want to return to the company, or one of your current coworkers may move to your new company.

What to Do If You Are Terminated

Sometimes, the choice to leave a job is not your own. You may be **terminated**. This is the term most businesses use when they fire an employee. There are two types of termination: for cause and due to circumstances beyond your control.

Being terminated **for cause** means being fired for violation of a policy or law. In most companies, violations such as using alcohol or illegal drugs at work, physically threatening or harming another employee, or stealing company property are grounds for **immediate dismissal**. This means termination without any advance notice.

Termination for poor performance may take place over time. Most companies give an employee one or more chances to improve their performance within a specific time period. In this case, the supervisor is required to document, put in writing, the performance problems and remedies. This enables the company to show that it has treated the employee with fairness prior to termination. Organizations that have a unionized workforce may also have to abide by procedures spelled out in the union contract.

Another type of termination is due to circumstances beyond your control. Many companies hire employees with the understanding that employment can be terminated at any time and for no specific reason. This is called **at-will employment**. The employee or the employer has the right to terminate employment at any time.

When a company is in financial trouble or is bought or sold, the result is often the termination of many people at the same time. When employees are terminated because positions have been cut, the term used is **layoff**. Another term for this is **reduction in force (RIF)**. Employees affected by these situations may feel angry, sad, or depressed. These are typical responses, but the situation will be even more serious if it is not handled with a constructive attitude. The constructive response is to start looking for a new job.

*Dragon Images/
Shutterstock.com*

Apply

Case: Dealing with a Layoff

You are an employee who is highly valued by your manager. In your six months on the job, you have received excellent feedback. You love your job, have a good relationship with your coworkers, and plan to work in this company for a long time. Unfortunately, budget cutbacks cause a layoff. Although you are an ideal employee, you are also the newest person hired. Your company has a layoff policy based on **seniority**, which means terminations are based on length of service. Thus, the newest workers are terminated first. The worker who will be assuming your duties is not as capable as you are. You are angry and frustrated.

Case Analysis

1. List three options for dealing with your job situation.

_____
_____
_____
_____
_____
_____
_____
_____
_____

2. List the option you would choose, and explain why you would choose it.

_____
_____
_____
_____
_____
_____
_____
_____
_____
_____
_____
_____
_____
_____

Review

True or False

Indicate *T* if the statement is true or *F* if the statement is false.

1. _____People usually change jobs after two years.

2. _____Some people stay at a job they do not like because of fear of the unknown.

3. _____Loyalty to the worker's current employer is a good reason to stay at a job.

4. _____Dreading going to work is one clue that it may be time to look for a new job.

5. _____When looking for a new job, an employee does *not* have to put any effort into the current job.

6. _____Being fired for cause means the employee is subject to immediate dismissal.

7. _____When a worker has accepted a new job, the resignation should be submitted to the supervisor in writing.

8. _____It is okay to say you are unhappy with your current company after accepting a new job.

9. _____Many people become angry, sad, or depressed when they lose a job.

10. _____If you are terminated because of a layoff, it is the same as being fired for cause.

Check Your Understanding

1. List six to eight clues that should encourage you to consider looking for a new job.

_____

_____

_____

_____

_____

_____

_____

2. If you experience any of the clues, does that mean you should leave your job immediately? Explain your answer.

_____

_____

_____

_____

_____

3. Why should you *not* use your current employer's resources when you look for a new job?

_____

_____

_____

_____

_____

_____

4. Describe a positive way to leave a job.

_____

_____

_____

_____

_____

_____

_____

_____

Journal Writing

1. Think of the groups or activities in which you participate, such as a course, club, team, or job. Have you ever had to leave one of them? If yes, describe how you left and whether the experience was positive. If no, describe how you would leave in a positive manner.

_____

_____

_____

_____

_____

_____

_____

_____

_____

_____

_____

_____

_____

_____

2. Have you ever experienced *inertia*? Describe the situation and why you were not motivated to make changes. How did you overcome your inertia?

_____

_____

_____

_____

_____

_____

_____

_____

_____

_____

_____

_____

_____

_____

Glossary

A

absenteeism. Being absent from work. (16)

accepting responsibility. Being willing to answer for your actions and decisions. (11)

active listening. Carefully listening to what is being said, observing nonverbal cues, and responding with appropriate feedback. (12)

ageism. Prejudice based on age. (6)

aggressive behavior. Actions that are hostile or destructive. (9)

ambition. Desire for rank, fame, money, power, or a combination of these things. (18)

attitude. State of mind, belief, or feeling that causes a person to act or react in a certain way. (2)

at-will employment. Understanding that the employee or the employer has the right to terminate employment at any time and for no specific reason. (22)

B

bigot. Person who lacks tolerance for others who are different from them in some way. (6)

body language. Communication that uses gestures, facial expressions, and actions; another term for *nonverbal communication*. (1, 12)

C

career goal. Clearly defined objective that identifies the specific job or career path a person wishes to achieve. (18)

career path. Move from one job to another to reach a career goal. (17)

career plateau. Period in a career when an employee feels unable to make progress. (17)

common courtesy. Polite behavior and good etiquette, such as saying "please" and "thank you." (20)

communication. Process of sending messages from one person to another and receiving feedback. (1, 12)

company policies. Written rules of conduct within an organization outlining the responsibilities of both employees and the employer. (15)

Note: The number in parentheses following each definition indicates the chapter in which the term can be found.

company procedures. Work guidelines and processes that may be written or unwritten. (15)

competition. Rivalry between two or more people who are trying to reach the same goal. (20)

confidential information. Private information intended for selected individuals. (10)

conscientiousness. Quality of being committed to doing what is right and proper. (13)

consequences. Results of an action or behavior. (11)

constructive attitude. Attitude that combines being positive with taking action to get results. (7)

constructive criticism. Feedback given to help someone improve or learn something. (21)

cooperation. Working together for the common good. (3)

coworkers. People who work together within a department or work group and others with whom they interact in the workplace. (4)

criticism. Expression of disapproval or the act of pointing out problems or faults with something or someone. (21)

D

defensive. Refusing to accept responsibility for mistakes and attempting to justify the actions. (21)

dependability. Quality of doing what you say you will do and following through on promises or commitments. (13)

destructive criticism. Feedback intended to inflict hurt. (21)

direct reports. Staff members who work under the authority of the managers and supervisors; also called *subordinates*. (4)

disciplinary action. Formal response to misbehavior or rule breaking at work; may be a verbal warning, a written warning, a suspension, or termination. (16)

discrimination. Negative actions targeted at individuals based on their race, nationality, religion, gender, or sexual orientation. (6)

dissatisfaction. State of being unhappy and seeing the negative side of things. (6)

F

favoritism. Special attention shown to someone in a group of people who are all supposed to be treated equally. (5)

flextime. Policy that allows workers to vary their arrival and departure within a specified time period at the start and end of the workday. (16)

for cause. Being terminated for violation of a policy or law. (22)

G

giving notice. Telling your supervisor that you intend to leave your job. (22)

goal setting. Procedure that requires the supervisor and each worker to agree on the employee's performance objectives. (15)

good character. Integrity; being dependable, loyal, trustworthy, honest, and conscientious. (13)

good judgment. Ability to make good decisions. (13)

goodwill. Positive feeling that occurs when someone does something that benefits you. (7)

group mentality. Tendency of the people in a group to think and behave in ways that conform. (2, 10)

H

hierarchy. Ranking of workers based on the level of their jobs. (4)

honesty. Quality of telling the truth and being trustworthy. (13)

human relations. Interaction of people with each other. (1)

human relations skills. Skills used to make interactions with people as positive as possible. (1)

I

immediate dismissal. Termination without any advance notice. (22)

impartial. Not showing favoritism or taking sides. (4)

inertia. Lacking motivation to make changes. (22)

initiative. Quality of self-motivation—ability to get the job done on your own. (13)

integrity. Good character; being dependable, loyal, trustworthy, honest, and conscientious. (13)

interact. To engage with others through communication and behavior. (1)

J

jealousy. Feeling of hostility toward someone believed to be a rival or toward someone perceived to be getting special treatment or advantages. (5)

job performance. Assessment of how well employees perform their job duties and what areas need improvement or development. (5)

job satisfaction. Degree to which employees enjoy their work and feel a sense of achievement. (5)

L

layoff. Termination of employees because positions have been cut; another term for *reduction in force*. (22)

loyalty. Quality of giving support and having a sense of duty toward someone or something. (13)

M

manager. Person who manages the work of one or more employees. (5)

mentor. Person with experience who supports and advises someone with less experience to help them develop. (5, 18)

merit. Actual quality of work. (5)

miscommunication. Failure to communicate adequately and properly. (12, 20)

misinformation. Untrue or incomplete information. (10)

misunderstanding. Argument resulting from the failure of two people to understand each other. (20)

mixed message. Communication where words and body language conflict. (1)

morale. Feelings and attitudes among employees about their work and the workplace. (8)

motive. Reason that explains a person's actions. (10)

mutually rewarding relationship. Relationship that is beneficial to everyone involved. (20)

N

negative attitude. Focusing on the bad aspects of interactions and situations. (2)

negative reinforcement. Encouragement of negative attitudes. (9)

networking. Means of connecting with people and establishing relationships that help achieve one's career goals. (18)

nonverbal communication. Communication without words; also called *body language*. (1, 12)

O

observational learning. Watching someone to learn how to do something. (13)

on-the-job training. Training designed to familiarize new employees with the specific skills, processes, and procedures required for the job. (15)

opportunity. New set of circumstances that makes it possible to do or learn something. (14)

optimistic. Believing that, for the most part, life is good and expecting good things to happen. (2)

organizational culture. Values, behavioral expectations, and practices that guide and inform the actions of employees. (15, 16)

orientation. Program to provide information to new employees about the organization, its mission, and its policies. (15)

overqualified. Having more knowledge and skills than a job requires. (8)

oversensitive/oversensitivity. Being too easily upset, angered, or offended; taking slights and mistakes too personally or seriously. (4, 6)

P

paid leave. Time off with pay; may include vacation, sick leave, and time off for certain holidays or personal business. (16)

peers. People who work at the same job level. (4)

perfectionist. Someone who wants to do everything perfectly and dreads making a mistake. (19)

performance goals; performance objectives. Specific projects or work tasks that an employee is expected to achieve within a set period of time. (5, 15)

performance review. Formal evaluation of an employee's work and productivity. (15)

personality conflict. Discord between people caused by their different temperaments. (20, 22)

personality traits. Relatively stable, consistent, and enduring characteristics that form a person's patterns of behaviors, attitudes, and feelings. (2)

pessimistic. Believing that in most cases the worst is likely to happen. (2)

positive attitude. Looking on the bright side of situations and interactions with people. (2)

prejudice. Hostility toward a group of people based on external characteristics, such as race, gender, or age. (6)

prioritizing. Managing the order of importance of various aspects of your work and personal life. (14)

proactive. Taking action to make changes or solve problems rather than reacting to things that happen. (7)

probation period. Period of time during which an employee is hired, but performance is evaluated to determine if employment will be permanent. (15)

productivity. Measure of efficiency as defined by the organization's expectations of its workforce. (3)

professional organizations. Groups established to help people be successful in their chosen profession. (18)

pros and cons. Arguments for and against something. (13)

R

racism. Prejudice based on race or ethnicity. (6)

rapport. Friendly, harmonious relationship that makes communication easy and productive. (20)

reduction in force (RIF). Termination of employees because positions have been cut; another term for *layoff*. (22)

reliable. Being trusted and depended on to keep one's obligations. (16)

resign. To voluntarily leave a position. (22)

rumor. Widely spread information whose truth and source are unknown to the people who pass it around. (10)

rumor mill. Process in which people hear a rumor and pass it on, often adding misinformation. (10)

S

self-awareness. Being aware of yourself and the reactions of others. (1)

self-confidence. Feeling sure of yourself and secure in your ability to handle challenges or succeed at something. (8, 14)

self-esteem. Measure of how you feel about yourself. (14)

selfishness. Trait of people who have the attitude that their needs and concerns are more important than those of others. (6)

seniority. System of basing terminations on employees' length of service. (22)

service industry. Industry consisting of businesses that provide a service, such as restaurants, hotels, airlines, salons, mass transportation, and medical care. (6)

sexism. Prejudice based on gender. (6)

skill. Ability that requires development through study and practice. (3)

status quo. Current state of affairs and how things are routinely done. (15)

stress. Feeling of general anxiety, mental tension, or emotional distress. (9)

stressors. Causes of stress. (9)

subordinates. Staff members who work under the authority of the managers and supervisors; also called *direct reports*. (4, 5)

supervisor. Person who manages the work of one or more employees. (5)

T

talent. Unique pattern and combination of abilities. (3)

tardiness. Arriving late to work. (16)

team. Group of people who work together for a common goal. (3)

team player. Worker who acts to help the team succeed as a whole. (3)

teamwork. Activity of people working together to produce results that achieve the organization's goals. (3)

terminated. Business term for firing an employee. (22)

trade secret. Confidential information that people within the company must know, but which they do not want people outside the company to know. (10)

trustworthy. Being deserving of trust or confidence. (13)

U

unprofessional. Acting in ways that do not meet the high standards of an excellent worker. (16)

unwritten rules. Guidelines for behavior that employees know because they are a part of the organizational culture, although not a part of the written company policies. (15)

V

values. Standards used for evaluating people and events and for making decisions about what is important. (2)

verbal aggression. Speaking in a hostile or angry way. (9)

verbal communication. Communication using words. (1, 12)

W

work attitude. Attitude toward work that has three components: attitude toward self, attitude toward work (work ethic), and attitude toward the workplace. (14)

work ethic. Person's attitude that attaches a moral value to hard work; work ethic may be strong or weak. (14)

written resignation. Notification stating an employee's intention to leave a job and the date of the last day of employment. (22)

Index

Constructive criticism, 227
Cooperation, 33
Coworker relationships, 40–49
    characteristics of a good relationship, 43
    communication, 45
    effect on others, 44
    new worker, 166
    problems, 44
    taking responsibility, 44–45
    types, 43
Coworkers, definition, 43
Criticism, 224–233
    accepting, 227–228
    criticizing others, 228
    definition, 227
    handling, 227
    learning from, 227–228

D

Defensive, 227
Dependability, 143
Destructive attitudes, 64–75
    counteracting, 69
    discrimination, 67–68
    dissatisfaction, 69
    effect on productivity, 67
    oversensitivity, 68
    prejudice, 67–68
    selfishness, 68
    stress and, 99
Destructive criticism, 227
Direct report, 43
Disciplinary action, 175
Discrimination, 68
Dissatisfaction, 69

E

Emergencies and time off, 177

F

Favoritism, 55
Flextime, 175
For cause, 239 *See also* Terminated

G

Giving notice, 238
Goals
    performance, 53
    setting, 166, 195
Good character, 143
Good judgment, 144
    thinking through pros and cons, 144
Goodwill, 79
Group mentality, 24, 112

H

Hierarchy, 43
Honesty, 144
Human relations, 11
Human relations skills, 8–17
    communication, 11–12
    definition, 11
    influence on job success, 12
    need for, 11
    self-awareness, 12

I

Immediate dismissal, 239 *See also* Terminated
Impartial, 44
Inertia, 238
Initiative, 144
    career progress and, 196
Integrity, 143 *See also* Good character
Interact, 11

J

Jealousy, 54
Job, leaving, 234–243 *See also* Leaving a job
Job performance, 53
Job satisfaction, 53
Job skills
    communication, 133
    human relations, 12
    repairing damaged relationships, 218
    teamwork, 33–34